THE DEATH OF THE PAST

By the same author

THE DEATH
OF THE PAST

J. H. PLUMB

With a Preface by Simon Schama and
an Introduction by Niall Ferguson

First published 1969 by Macmillan Press Ltd.
This edition published 2004 by
PALGRAVE MACMILLAN
Houndmills, Basingstoke, Hampshire RG21 6XS and
175 Fifth Avenue, New York, N.Y. 10010
Companies and representatives throughout the world

PALGRAVE MACMILLAN is the global academic imprint of the Palgrave
Macmillan division of St. Martin's Press, LLC and of Palgrave Macmillan Ltd.
Macmillan® is a registered trademark in the United States, United Kingdom
and other countries. Palgrave is a registered trademark in the European
Union and other countries.

ISBN 10: 1–4039–0698–X paperback
ISBN 13: 978-1-4039-0698-4 paperback

This book is printed on paper suitable for recycling and made from
fully managed and sustained forest sources. Logging, pulping and
manufacturing processes are expected to conform to the
environmental regulations of the country of origin.

A catalogue record for this book is available from the British Library.

Library of Congress Cataloging-in-Publication Data
Plumb, J. H. (John Harold), 1911–
    The death of the past / J.H. Plumb.—2nd ed.
        p. cm.
    Includes bibliographical references and index.
    ISBN 1–4039–0698–X (pbk.)
        1. Historiography. 2. History—Philosophy. I. Title.

D13.P55 2003
907'.2—dc21   2002193082

Transferred to Digital Printing 2009

FOR
JOHN BURROW

CONTENTS

FOREWORD:
J.H. PLUMB

Simon Schama

The past may or may not have been dead when
J.H. Plumb pronounced its obsequies, but to those
of us who were taught by him in Cambridge in
the 1960s, the author was unforgettably, alarm-
ingly, alive. Whatever stereotypes those of us
arriving at Christ's College in 1963 might have
had about history dons, a first encounter with Jack
Plumb in his rooms – a small man with a perfectly round, bald head, seated in a big armchair,
nattily dressed in three-piece, crisply tailored suit,
a high-coloured Jermyn Street striped shirt, and
bow tie – swiftly saw off the cliché of tweeds and
amontillado. Display cases poured brilliant light
on to Sèvres porcelain in kingfisher blue and rose
pink. The walls were filled with Dutch still-life
and genre paintings: a young man with a weak
chin and get-me whiskers; a mournful bar-girl
with too much sallow cleavage; an arrangement
for hock and lemons. Not a bottle of sherry to be
seen, but decanters of Chateau Figeac, often.
When Plumb spoke, and especially when he
chuckled as he often did, the effect of Voltaire in

the Fens was complete. But there was, however, a serious price to be paid for all this epicurean dazzlement bestowed on clever but slightly stunned youth: intellectual survival under intense and unsparing fire.

Plumb was famously, tigerishly, combative; though also affable and witty, his conversation was punctuated by bursts of laughter at the follies of humanity past and present, of which academia itself, he made clear, offered the richest trove. His temper was naturally quizzical, sardonic, gleeful. But it was impossible, amid the gales of irony that swept through the room on the subject of some hapless figure, not to be nervous that one might be next for the Treatment. The slightly exopthalmic eyes which glittered from behind his spectacles would fix steadily and expectantly on whomever a Plumb question, joke or challenge alighted. Abashed thoughtfulness was not a possible response, nor was any sort of laboured earnestness. Anyone suspected of Being Serious About Religion was subjected to a Philosophical barrage of teasing which could sometimes turn punishingly picador. Most of the wounding, though, happened in the intense hour or so of history supervisions in those rooms, when we read our essays, our hearts sinking to our boots should Jack begin to fidget ominously in the yellow-upholstered armchair. When it went well, the praise was fulsome and went straight to our giddy heads like champagne. But for some, it seldom did go well. Come six in the evening, the remains of large undergraduates (for this was then a rugby college) could be seen collapsed in trembling exhaustion in the College Buttery after an unhappy hour with Plumb, dosing themselves with healing pints of Watney's, repenting solecisms uttered on the Merovingians (for Plumb loved teaching outside his speciality) and swearing never to go through it again.

But of course we always did. There was, for a start, always the prospect of the occasional magical supervision, when he would spend a half an hour analysing the form, as well as the content of a paragraph or two; juggling, like the nimblest editor, with the rhetorical structure of the essay, suggesting how it could gain more punch and conviction were paragraph four to have been the opening and so on. Towards the end, sometimes over those hard-earned glasses of claret, an encyclopedic range of bibliographic suggestions would tumble out; many of them eccentrically original. A tentative essay on the cultural backwash of the discovery of the New World drew from him amazement that I had read neither Redcliffe Salaman's *History of the Potato*, nor Godefroy Atkinson's *Nouveaux Horizons de la Renaissance française,* the latter a

book which lived up to the winning peculiarity
of its author's name by tackling Montaigne and
the *Pléiade* via a lengthy discussion of the implications of Indian nudity on the theology of the
Catholic reform movement.

Our own trials by fire culminated in the ritual
of the Plumb after-dinner seminar. The serious-
ness of the event was marked by its being con-
vened, not in the sitting room, but on the other
side of the stairs of 'O' staircase, in Jack's dining
room. A Sheraton table, the polish high enough
for us to see our fretful faces embarrassingly
reflected, was laid with a tall Paul de Lamerie
silver candelabrum. Silver bowls brimmed with
fruit including a strangely incongruous banana.
Two decanters of claret rested on the sideboard
which, once the speaker had finished his paper,
would be brought to the table to do the rounds.
For forty minutes or so either Roy Porter,
Geoffrey Parker, Andrew Wheatcroft, John
Barber or I would hammer and stammer
through our stuff, each of using whatever kind of
rhetorical persuasiveness we could muster amid
the intimidating antiques. Roy's speciality was
jokes at which he'd be the first to chortle (and
they were usually very funny). Geoffrey Parker
fortified himself with armour of unassailable and
esoteric scholarship. Schama, as usual depended
overmuch on adjectival overload and over-

wrought atmospherics to conceal the shakiness of his hypotheses. (*Plus ça change.*) In the candle-lit glow one always knew if things were going well. JHP's not twanging an elastic band, for instance, was definitely a good sign, as was his not turning his chair sideways to commune with the smirking likeness of Sir Robert Walpole on the wall.

After the reading came the listeners' turn to respond, or else. The claret and fruit circulated (Porter and I usually doing unspeakable things with the grape scissors, an instrument for which London lower-middle-class life had inadequately prepared us). The diplomatic psychology of the discussion was tricky: too fierce in our criticism and we would sacrifice a friendship; too cosy or indulgent, then we risked disbelief and raillery from Plumb. So we generally told the truth. At the end of the circle of comments, Jack would supply his own, and belie his reputation for fierceness by generous helpings of praise for the student's research and his grip on the subject, even while raising questions about both evidence and analysis which not infrequently turned the whole exercise inside out and upside down. Whatever else happened in those seminars, we all learned the art of vigilantly sympathetic atten-tiveness, which has stood me, at any rate, in good stead in over thirty years of teaching.

But aside from pedagogic style, was there a 'Plumb' philosophy of history, evident in these bracing hours of instruction, and faithfully represented in *The Death of the Past*? In the mid 1960s, it seemed to be an obligation for every historian worth his salt to make some sort of utterance on what history was and wasn't, many of them in response to and in exasperated refutation of E.H. Carr's *What is History?*, a book which its countless critics (all of them in the right) see as the mailed fist of determinism lurking in the velvet glove of a faux-scepticism. Herbert Butterfield, G.R. Elton (Plumb's particular nemesis); and many others had all put their methodological oars in, but what is striking about so many of these *professions de foi* is their un-self-examined address to the converted. Their working assumption – fair enough in the 1960s, when the escalator from A-level history to undergraduate history to graduate history to that first Research Fellowship was serenely uninterrupted by anything resembling a power outage from the employment *zeitgeist* – was that academic history would continue to be the dominant discipline of both the humanities and the social sciences; its scholarly *gravitas* weightier than the study of literature yet somehow more imaginatively creative then sociology or economics. For Elton, the question 'Who cares?' would have been not so much impertinent as unthinkable. The issue was not to legitimize the discipline so much as to issue a stringent manual for its professional practice.

For the worldly Plumb, though, with his relish for, and brilliance at, popular history writing and journalism, especially in America, where he was the leading literary light of *Horizon* magazine, there was no question of history resting smugly on its laurels. Trapped inside the professional stockade, he believed, history would atrophy into an arid scholasticism. 'What do they of history know' I remember him borrowing from E.M. Forster (who had in turn creatively pilfered Kipling) 'who know only other historians?' For Plumb, history was either a public craft or it was nothing; and in this spirit he was constantly urging on us books he cherished which had been written by historians either rejected by the academy or who had chosen to work outside it. Iris Origo's *Merchant of Prato*, Barbara Tuchman's *The Guns of August* and Frances Yates's work on neo-Platonist hermetics (very much an eccentricity in the 1960s) all come to mind. While others cringed at the belletrism they imputed to C.V. Wedgwood, Plumb welcomed her to High Table and introduced us personally to that elegant, surprisingly astringent mind.

The battle lines were decisively drawn for us

at Christ's: the encyclopedic and the omnivorous (us) versus the arid and the parochial (them); history seen as an inquiry into the human condition (us) versus history assumed to be the unfolding epic of English (not even British) governing institutions (them), history which embraced the literary and the imaginative without ever forsaking the hard tests of documentary evidence (us), versus history which treated strong writing as a fig-leaf for analytical mushiness (them). And while Plumb was adamant about the indispensability of the archive, neither did he fetishise it. He insisted that the archive startlingly anticipated Arlette Farge and Pierre Bourdieu; that it was a social institution, with its own invented practices, hierarchies of significance, both human and documentary and which was as much the product of a particular culture as its shaper. *Caveat lector!*

The notion that the historian's task consisted entirely of archaeological self-effacement before the bedrock of archival truth, being a mole-like digger of nuggets and gobbets, he found not so much professionally deluded as betraying an almost pathetic want of critical self-consciousness.

Yet it was precisely Plumb's abiding and unapologetic sense that history lived for others not just for itself; that it was, at root, a civic vocation not a monastic profession, which snared him in all kinds of contradictions, some of which are exposed, others glossed over in *The Death of the Past*. The central message of the book – that history, practised as a truly critical discipline, was the enemy of a 'past' in which liberty of thought and action were forever in thrall to the claimed authority of ancestral prescription – actually pointed its readers in two directions at once. On the one hand, history, construed as the study of human society, needed the input of professionals saturated in and invigorated by the methodologies of the *Annales* school, especially Marc Bloch and Fernand Braudel, if it were to break free simultaneously from a culture of sentimental deference to heritage and from the airless claustrophobia of Gobbet-Land. On the other hand, none of that would make any difference to the survival of history as a public craft, unless that new professionalism could be translated into genuinely popular writing. In principle, there was no reason why this little miracle should not happen, and Plumb's ambitious multi-volume *History of Human Society* attempted to do just that. But as an advertisement for a new, yet genuinely popular history, the series never really took off, not least because the quality of its writing, while seldom exactly pedestrian, never really made for page-turning either. The project, stalled before its ambitions could be realised, remained obstinately encyclopedic rather than genuinely innovative. Several volumes only brought home the truism that Braudels, Blochs and Fèbvres, capable of achieving a synthesis of narrative and social analysis of ethnography and textual exegesis, were painfully scarce. Narrative drive and the force of events – precisely the history repudiated by Braudel as the artifice of dull practitioners in favour of the slow heave and shift of tectonic-plate forces – were in fact the *sine qua non* of bringing readers back to history and thus liberating them from 'the past'.

And Plumb, a supremely accomplished narrator, knew this. However much he may have asserted the equivalence of the history of the potato with the history of the British (or American) Civil Wars, in his heart of hearts he didn't believe it. In fact, at the height of the mode for social history in the *Annales* style, Plumb could be found insisting on the power of speech-acts to shake and shape the destiny of communities and nations. If, in some of his great lecture performances (as in his work on Walpole) he might suggest that parliamentary rhetoric was a veil behind which the grind of monied interest did its business, on other days he would impersonate the histrionics of a Fox or a Chatham with precisely the opposite conclusion in mind.

His considering intellect, then, may have pointed him away from the power of argument and ideology; but the vitality of his temperament and his deep engagement with the mystery of language, pointed, always, towards it. That, indeed, was the gravamen of his ferocious argument against Lewis Namier, whose obsession with interest over ideology Plumb thought a myopic mistake about how humans actually behave.

None of which prevented Plumb from accomplishing an important and even lasting little polemic in *The Death of the Past*. But as so often with him (as with many of the finest historians) what he says is less significant than the way that he says it. Though Plumb clung to the notion that history had to be more than just the exercise of the pleasure principle; more than merely the inspection of the generations of humanity; that it ought, really, to bring about some sort of epistemological and cultural alteration; he was actually hard-pressed to define what such an alteration might be. While all his pupils would agree that a world without, not only a sense of the past, but critical history, would be dangerously worse off, in the end, Plumb, like many of us, remained stymied by an aesthetic in search of a didactic.

INTRODUCTION[1]

Niall Ferguson

The Death of the Past Personified

The case of the patient 'H.M.' is well known to specialists in neural science. An otherwise intelligent young man, H.M. suffered from epilepsy. In August 1953 – at a time when neurology was still in its infancy – a surgeon performed an operation on him known as a 'bilateral medial temporal lobe resection', removing tissue from the medial basal regions of the brain. The operation was supposed to reduce the patient's susceptibility to seizures. It did. Unfortunately, it had two disastrous side effects. First, it destroyed eleven years of his memory: although he was operated on when he was 27, H.M. could subsequently recollect nothing that had happened to him after the age of 16. Secondly, and much

---

[1] I should declare an interest – or rather acknowledge a debt. Although Jack Plumb never taught me – I went to the wrong university for that – it was largely as a result of his influence that I began my academic career as a research fellow at Christ's College, Cambridge. We had never met, but he had read some draft chapters of my doctoral thesis, and approved. That approval was enough to secure my election. From the time I arrived at Christ's – in the autumn of 1989 – until Jack's death in 2001 he was an unfailingly generous friend and mentor.

more seriously, the operation destroyed his ability *to* remember, so that he became incapable of re-collecting for more than a few minutes anything that he experienced subsequent to the operation.[2] One of the many medical studies of H.M.'s case describes what this meant in practice:[3]

> Ten months after the operation, the family moved to a new house which was situated only a few blocks away from their old one, on the same street. When examined . . . nearly a year later, H.M. had not yet learned the new address, nor could he be trusted to find his way home alone. . . . The patient will do the same jigsaw puzzles day after day without showing any practice effect, and read the same magazines over and over again without finding their contents familiar.[3]

The consensus among the many researchers who have studied the case is that the over-zealous surgeon had unwittingly removed parts of the brain crucial to the human capacity to recall past events.[4]

---

[2] Deniz Yuret, 'Patient H. M.', Ohio State University Psychology department case notes (Sept. 1995).

[3] Brenda Milner, 'Description of Amnesia Patient H.M.' in Floyd E. Bloom, *Brain, Mind, and Behavior*, 2nd edn (New York, 1988), pp. 254, 256.

[4] To be precise, the hippocampus, the amygdala, the parahip-pocampus and the entorhinal cortex.

The extreme form of amnesia which afflicted H.M. provides a vivid illustration of what Sir John Plumb meant by 'the death of the past'. For H.M. the past after 1942 was almost entirely dead,[5] both as an accumulation of recollected events and as a process of memorization. To grasp what Plumb was driving at in this book, all one need do is to imagine an entire society in the condition of H.M.

Plumb himself knew that the past could be amended – and improved upon – by history. His own life illustrated perfectly how that process worked: born the son of humble 'clicker' in a Leicester shoe factory, he transformed himself in the course of a long and distinguished academic career into a courtier and connoisseur, the familiar not only of Windsors and Rothschilds but also of the more ancient and generally more aloof dynasties of the English aristocracy. No amount of Sèvres porcelain or *premier cru* Lafite could entirely efface Plumb's past, however. On the contrary, he liked nothing better than to point out that his worldly achievements were 'a long way from Somerville Road, Leicester'. In Plumb's eyes, an individual could only advance as long as he retained knowledge of his past, and the same applied to societies. 'What matters', he

---

[5] With a few notable exceptions: he had heard of rock music, astronauts and the assassination of John F. Kennedy.

once declared at the height of a political row at his beloved Christ's College, 'is the academic leadership to ensure that the College survives and prospers as it has done for the last five hundred years.'[6] The death of the past – meaning the abnegation of those five centuries of academic achievement – would mean the death of the College's future.

★

If ever an entire society seemed intent on killing its own past off, then it was the society to which this book was originally addressed. Based on four lectures Plumb gave in New York in March 1968, *The Death of the Past* bears the distinct imprint of its time. That same month, there were race riots in Memphis, Tennessee, where Martin Luther King Jr would be assassinated on 4 April. The North Vietnamese Tet offensive was in full swing and American support for the war was ebbing: March 1968 was also the month of the My Lai massacre, when American soldiers killed over four hundred men, women and children, though the atrocity was not made public until over a year later. Student unrest was simmering

---

[6] Neil McKendrick, 'Sir John Plumb: A Biographical Memoir', unpublished manuscript, Cambridge 2002. I am deeply grateful to the author for permission to quote from this revelatory text, as well as for his comments on an earlier version of this introduction.

on both sides of the Atlantic. Even as Plumb prepared his lectures, the Beatles were winning a Grammy Award for *Sergeant Pepper's Lonely Hearts Club Band*; the Rolling Stones were about to release 'Jumpin' Jack Flash'. Rarely have traditional attitudes and structures seemed as ripe for interment as they did in the spring of '68. The past was never more moribund.

Himself a man of the Left until his dotage, Plumb was of course alive to the revolutionary mood; it was detectable even in Cambridge and quite unmistakable in New York. So it is not surprising to find allusions here to both the Civil Rights movement and the sexual revolution. Note, for example, his long footnote about the 'white' character of mainstream American historiography, whereas 'the last two years have witnessed a determination amongst the blacks to acquire a past of their own'. 'The sanctions of the past [that] lay heavily on marriage . . . are rapidly crumbling,' he remarks later. 'The same is true of other sexual activity. . . . Biological urges, compulsive needs, statistically proved, guide us to toleration and, perhaps, back to our humanity. The taboos of the dead no longer cast their shadows across the bed.'

Yet these signs of the swinging times are not really what Plumb means by the 'death of the past'. Rather, the question he addresses here is one which is as important today as it was thirty-five years ago. It is whether or not academic history, in dismantling our received notions about the past, is essentially a destructive enterprise, capable of dislodging but incapable of replacing the largely mythical but socially functional 'past'. In worrying about the antagonism between a past which enhanced social cohesion and a consciously revisionist history produced by professionals, Plumb was in many ways prescient.[7] Though his balding, besuited and bespectacled figure could scarcely have been less trend-setting in 1968, The Death of the Past was – in some respects – intellectually ahead of its time.

The Cambridge Context

To understand what is novel about *The Death of the Past*, it is necessary to understand not only its political context, but – more importantly – its academic context. This also helps illuminate what is *not* novel about it.

Plumb wrote his New York lectures when he was at the height of his very considerable powers as an historian. He was 56. Only a year before he had published *The Growth of Political Stability in England, 1675–1725*, which originated as a bril-

[7] See most recently Jonathan Clark, *Our Shadowed Present: Modernism, Postmodernism and History* (London, 2003).

liant series of Ford lectures in Oxford. He had begun the 1960s by publishing the second of his two volumes on the life of Sir Robert Walpole. If he had made his reputation as a meticulous portraitist (Walpole had been preceded by Chatham in 1953), by the late 1960s he felt ready to wield a broader brush. Although universally acknowledged as the world's leading authority on eighteenth-century England, he had deliberately (some would say over-ambitiously) stretched himself by studying and then teaching Chinese history. Politically, too, Plumb felt himself secure, if not yet quite at the top of the academic greasy pole. Long one of the dominant personalities at Christ's, he had been elected to a personal chair at Cambridge in 1966 and, at the time of his trip to New York, held the powerful position of chairman of the History Faculty Board. A fellowship of the British Academy was impending. He and his arch-rival Geoffrey Elton (who would ultimately beat him to what seemed the most glittering prize of all, the Regius Chair of Modern History) seemed, at worst, to be neck and neck.

Though neither could be classed as a major contributor to the philosophy of history, Plumb and Elton were (or appeared to be) growing apart rapidly in their attitudes towards its practice. A year before, Elton had indeed published a book with the title *The Practice of History*, a kind of manifesto for his own brand of Anglicized German historicism: the application of Rankean methods of archival research to the traditional questions of English constitutional history. Plumb was bored by this. G.M. Trevelyan's one and only research student shared his supervisor's instinctive enthusiasm for social history and sensed – correctly – that it would be the social historians who would set the scholarly pace in the decades that lay ahead. As early as 1955 Plumb had declared (in his introduction to *Studies in Social History*) that 'social history, in the fullest and deepest sense of the term, is now a field of study of incomparable richness and the one in which the greatest discoveries will be made in this generation'.[8] In this same spirit, Plumb avers in *The Death of the Past* that 'The purpose of historical investigation is to produce answers, in the form of concepts and generalizations, to the fundamental problems of historical change in the social activities of men.' To teach history is, quite simply, to teach people about 'the nature of social change'.

This was, of course, to side with the young – with whom Plumb sympathized as a matter of principle – against Elton's methodological con-

[8] J. H. Plumb (ed.), *Studies in Social History: A Tribute to G. M. Trevelyan* (London / New York, 1955) p. xiv.

servatism. In some respects, however, the distance between the two seems less wide today than it seemed at the time. On the fundamental question of the historian's duty to represent the past *wie es eigentlich gewesen* – as it actually was – Plumb was as much a Rankean as Elton, as the following passages make clear:

> . . . From the Renaissance onwards there has been a growing determination for historians to try and understand what happened, purely *in its own terms* and not in the service of religion or national destiny, or morality, or the sanctity of institutions. . . . The historian's growing purpose has been to see things *as they really were*. . . . True history [is] the attempt to see things *as they were*, irrespective of what conflict this might create with what the wise ones of one's own society make of the past. . . . The development of historical criticism [is] to see things *as they were* in their own time.[9]

Plumb and Elton had enemies in common too. Plumb's gratuitous side-swipe at F.R. Leavis in a footnote – 'Another refugee in a never-never land of the past . . . whose picture of nineteenth-century England is as totally unrealistic as it must be emotionally satisfying' – might equally well have come from the pen of Elton. The same

[9] Emphases added.

could perhaps be said of Plumb's denunciation, *en passant*, of Macaulay's 'coarse and obvious' mind. Indeed, Plumb could echo an even more self-consciously conservative historian – Herbert Butterfield, with whom he had also broken earlier in his career – in his assessment of the relationship between Christianity and Western historiography.[10] Himself an inveterate atheist, Plumb nevertheless recognized the existence of a distinctively Christian 'sense of narrative and of unfolding purpose'. In the West, he argues in *The Death of the Past*, 'the past acquired a dynamic, almost a propulsion, which it did not acquire elsewhere'. The explicit contrast he draws is with China. The Chinese, Plumb argues with the sublime confidence of the dilettante, were

> concerned solely with creating an educative past – subtle, complex, highly detailed, accurate in commission, but not history. . . . *What closed their minds to the historical problem was its absence.* For the Chinese scholar the past stretched out from his own time like the sea – ruffled here and there by storm and tempest, but limitless. . . . The European's past never possessed the coherence or the unity, the all-embracing certainty of the Chinese.[11]

[10] Herbert Butterfield, *The Origins of History*, ed. Adam Watson (London, 1981).

[11] Emphasis in original.

Plumb and the Liberal Tradition

Here, however, we begin to detect Plumb's true intellectual provenance; for here, in this blithe disparagement of the Orient – this caricature of a Confucian monotony – speaks the unmistakable voice of a nineteenth-century liberal. Plumb adopts much the same *de haut en bas* tone when dismissing not only Macaulay but also Livy, Tacitus, Baker, Holinshed, Fabyan, Bancroft and Bishop Stubbs as mere 'annalists'.

Plumb had no doubt that a methodological chasm separated modern academic historians from both 'the ancient Chinese sages' and the earlier Western writers of history from Tacitus to Macaulay (Gibbon alone excepted). What had passed for history before the advent of 'scientific' scholarship in the later nineteenth century had merely been written 'to serve the authority of the ruling powers'. This brings us to the very heart of Plumb's argument: his distinction between 'the past' and 'history'. 'The past', according to Plumb, is either informally, and therefore badly, remembered or deliberately misrepresented for some ulterior motive. 'The past', he writes, 'is always a created ideology with a purpose, designed to control individuals, or motivate societies, or inspire classes.' Throughout history, it has been used 'to justify . . . the subjection and exploitation of men and women'.

History, by contrast, is not only Ranke's revelation of the past 'as it actually was', in its own terms, for its own sake; it is also a part of the grand liberal design to advance the cause of human progress. 'The future of history', writes Plumb unhesitatingly, 'is to cleanse the story of mankind from those deceiving visions of a purposeful past.' This means going beyond merely setting the record straight; inferences for future conduct can and should be derived from historical study. Thus:

> The historian can describe what has happened and what, therefore, it may be imprudent to do. . . . There are human truths to be derived from history. . . . Any process which increases man's . . . chance of controlling himself and his environment, is well worth pursuing.

And:

> The historian's purpose . . . is to deepen understanding about men and society, not merely for its own sake, but in the hope that a profounder knowledge, a profounder awareness[,] will help to mould human attitudes and human actions.

These passages might have been written in 1896, not 1968. Compare, to give a single example, Lord Acton's claim, in his inaugural lecture at Cambridge, that scientific historical research was one of the motive forces of European progress:

> The universal spirit of investigation and discovery . . . did not cease to operate and withstood the recurring efforts of reaction, until . . . it at length prevailed. This . . . gradual passage . . . from subordination to independence is a phenomenon of primary import to us, because historical science has been one of its instruments. [12]

In other words, the historian was not only concerned to describe the inevitable triumph of progress; in doing so, he was actually contributing towards it. Plumb is making much the same point when he declares: 'The one truth of history [is] that the condition of mankind has improved. . . . Man's success has derived from his application of reason, whether this has been to technical or to social questions. And it is the duty of the historian to teach this, to proclaim it, to demonstrate it. . . .'

To readers of a postmodern disposition, such language must be positively shocking. Even those

[12] Lord Acton, 'Inaugural Lecture on the Study of History', in W. H. McNeill (ed.), *Essays in the Liberal Interpretation of History* (Chicago 1967), pp. 304f.

who would seek to defend the nineteenth-century verities against the postmodernist tide must flinch at the stark simplicity of Plumb's call to arms.[13] There is, of course, no harm in being reminded that there used to be senior figures in university history departments who genuinely believed in such things as human progress and the possibility of learning from the past. But that fact, though doubtless interesting, is not a sufficient argument for reprinting *The Death of the Past* – nor, indeed, for rereading it. When Plumb declares that the task of humanity is 'the resolution of the tensions and antipathies that exist within the human species', we must remember when he was writing. And when he calls on history 'to help us achieve our identity, not as Americans or Russians, Chinese or Britons, black or white, rich or poor, but as men', we must forgive him – much as we should probably forgive John Lennon for the equally trite lyrics of the song 'Imagine' – and endeavour to delve deeper.

The Seeds of Doubt

The real importance of *The Death of the Past* lies not in Plumb's quite conventional liberal claims for the redemptive power of 'scientific' history, but in his thinly concealed anxieties that such

[13] See, for example, Richard Evans, *In Defence of History* (London, 1997).

history may be an inadequate substitute for the past. 'The old past is dying', he proclaims, adding: 'May history step into its shoes. . . . ' But can it? Did it?

Though scathing of earlier generations of writers of history – as opposed to true historians – Plumb had a keen, if grudging, awareness of the value of the past they created. As he himself puts it, 'To be unconscious of our historical selves is fraught with dangers.' The past, in his sense, may not be as good as proper history, but is certainly better than nothing. Not all the social and political functions of the past are, after all, malign – a fact that can scarcely have been lost on a man who spent more than half his life as a fellow of a Cambridge college:

> The majority of men and women . . . need the dimension of time because they are conscious of it. They realize that they are a part of an historical process . . . [and] they require to know what the nature of this process has been and is. They need an historical past, objective and true. . . . Each one of us is an historical being, held in a pattern created by Time. . . .

This is precisely why the predicament of the patient known as 'H.M.' strikes us as so tragic. Although in no physical pain, for more than half

his life – roughly the same years Plumb spent sur-
rounded by the past at Christ's – he was deprived
of this sense of 'historical being'. The 'pattern
created by Time' simply vanished from his life.

That such a fate could also befall a whole
society is the possibility that haunts *The Death of
the Past*, lurking between the lines of Plumb's
liberal optimism. What makes the possibility so
very hard for him to confront is that history – in
his sense – could play the role of surgeon in the
case of H.M., slicing out those vital parts of our
collective consciousness which keep the past,
with all its imperfections, alive.

The image that Plumb himself chooses is a
revealing one. 'History', he writes, 'has burrowed
like a death-watch beetle in this great fabric of
the past, honeycombing the timbers and making
the structure ruinous.' Or, as he puts it in a later
passage, 'History, which is so deeply concerned
with the past, has, in a sense, helped to destroy it
as a social force. . . . ' Plumb's point is a straight-
forward but crucially important one. The academic historians have declared a kind of war on
traditional interpretations of the past and have
indeed waged it with such success that those
interpretations have lost much of their validity.
The scholars' motives have been entirely honourable. In Plumb's words, 'The historian of
today . . . cannot accept the interpretation of the

past of his immediate ancestors or even of the mass of society in which he lives. Crude ideological interpretations . . . are a violation of his discipline. . . . ' But have the historians been able to replace 'the past' with an equally satisfying but also *true* history of their own making? On the contrary, writes Plumb – and one wonders whom he had in mind – 'many historians . . . have taken refuge in the meaninglessness of history, in the belief that history can only make a personal . . . statement; [that] it is a game for professional players who make the rules'. The depressing truth, as Plumb obliquely acknowledges early in the book, is that history is weaker than the past. Its light is 'flickering and feeble'. It lacks the rhetorical and anecdotal structures – what Hayden White would christen 'meta-narratives' – that make the bad, old past so compelling; indeed, so memorable.

At the time he wrote *The Death of the Past*, Plumb – like so many academics of the time – proclaimed himself a socialist. Yet it is possible to discern even at this early stage the seeds of that later revulsion against the social consequences of socialism (and its ally, permissive liberalism) that would subsequently sprout into full-blown Thatcherism in the 1980s. Consider, for example, Plumb's remark that 'in this period of vast and rapid transition there is great danger of a failure to secure an ideology of social attitude that can be taught and acceptably transmitted from generation to generation. As the past dies . . . there is a danger of social incoherence. . . .' Just a couple of pages later, Plumb reverts to the same theme:

> Once the vice-like grip of the past is loosened in religion, in education, in economic activity, then a paralysis in social matters quickly sets in. It is not too wanton to see one result . . . in the decay of the family structure and the growing independence of adolescent life.

These are distinctly conservative sentiments, and anticipate much of his more rancorous conversation two decades later. A similar train of thought would transport more than a few of Plumb's contemporaries across the political spectrum rather sooner – one thinks of Kingsley Amis. Only a tiny number of his Cambridge colleagues, notably Maurice Cowling, had discerned all along that the liberal assault on traditional institutions and structures of thought might end in general disintegration rather than universal enlightenment.[14]

Plumb could also sense that academic history

[14] Maurice Cowling, *Religion and Public Doctrine in Modern England*, vol. III (Cambridge, 2001).

itself might not live long to enjoy its triumph over history. In a darkly prophetic passage, he warned: 'If the past is allowed to die, or, having died, a new one fails to be conceived, that will be the fate of history. Its place as an interpreter of man's destiny will be taken by the social sciences.' This was tantamount to saying that his initial distinction between history and the past might be a false dichotomy: without some widely disseminated sense of the past, academic history might simply peter out due to lack of public interest. When Plumb called for 'a compulsive sense of the value of men's past' he was acknowledging that a victory for history over the past would be Pyrrhic indeed.

★

Thirty-five years on, is the past dead? Not if the popularity of historical documentaries on television is anything to go by. Recent series like Simon Schama's *History of Britain* and David Starkey's *Six Wives of Henry VIII* have succeeded in attracting British audiences of between two and four million.[15] To be sure, such programmes may be said to exist at the confluence of the past and history, attracting audiences by appealing to their existing collective memory of Britain's past,

---

[15] By an irony that Plumb would have enjoyed more than Elton, the former was a Plumb pupil, the latter one of Elton's.

while trying simultaneously to introduce them to at least some of the findings of academic research. But it is hard to believe that there would be any audience at all for them if the past, in Plumb's sense, were truly dead.

The real malady may lie on the other side. It is academic history, not the past, which seems moribund in Britain. For one thing, the subject ceases to be compulsory after the age of 14, making Britain one of only two countries in Europe where it is not compulsory up until the statutory school leaving age (the other is Iceland). Little more than a third of British teenagers study the subject at GCSE. What is more, the amount of time pre-GCSE pupils devote to the subject is trifling – usually one hour a week. All this has taken its inevitable toll on History at A-level. Since 1992 the number of History A-level candidates has fallen by nearly 16 per cent. Almost twice as many pupils now take Social Science – precisely the shift Plumb dreaded.

The squeezing of History also manifests itself in the subjects British pupils are taught. In theory there is a wide range of options available at 'Key Stage 3', ranging from 'British History 1066–1500' to 'A world study after 1900'. In practice 51 per cent of GCSE candidates and an astonishing 80 per cent of A-level candidates study Nazi Germany. The rest seem to study

Tudor England. History in many schools has been boiled down to 'Hitler and the Henries'. All this is inevitably affecting the quantity and, more seriously, the quality of applicants for places to read History at British universities.[16]

Far from supplanting the past, history now threatens to take the past down with it. According to one recent survey, nearly a third of 11- to 18-year-olds are under the impression that Oliver Cromwell fought at the Battle of Hastings, and fewer than half know that Nelson's flagship at Trafalgar was called the *Victory*. No fewer than 30 per cent are blissfully unaware that the First World War was fought in the twentieth century. It is not surprising to find that young people are distinctly under-represented in the audiences for television history. Just 14 per cent of the audience for the Channel 4 series *Empire* was under the age of 35, while 60 per cent were 55 or older. The under-sixteens accounted for barely 3 per cent. The past may be alive in British popular culture, but it is ageing fast.

Could this have been foreseen in 1968? Probably not. But Plumb's *Death of the Past* addressed the right question. Were academic historians wise to disparage all memories of the past other than those certified as authentic by their

---

[16] See the recent survey in *BBC History Magazine* (July 2003).

own researches, in their own refereed journals and monographs? Might the destructive energies of revisionism not ultimately create a vacuum, rather than a new and improved past? If Plumb continued to hope that the past could be remade by the historians, he felt a sneaking suspicion that they might botch the job. A generation later, his nightmare of a society which has lost both its past and its history seems far from fanciful.

In addition to being the initials of the medical world's most intensively studied amnesiac, the letters 'H.M.' stand for – some readers may already have noticed the irony – 'His' or 'Her Majesty's'. That the monarchy provided the indispensable framework of Britain's past was something Jack Plumb well understood: his *Royal Heritage* (1977) was by far his most commercially successful book. But what price the past if our children think Cromwell fought at Hastings? And what hope for history, the subject to which Plumb dedicated most of his life, and which is supposed to introduce each new generation to its heritage, royal, noble and common? Who will remember what H.M. really stands for, if the past and history both end up dead?

These are thoughts that the modern reader of *The Death of the Past* is bound to ponder, as Jack Plumb would ponder them were he alive and well today.

PREFACE

This book is based on the Saposnekow Lectures which I gave at the City College, New York, in March 1968, an honour which I greatly appreciated. I have decided to publish them very much as I gave them. They could easily have been extended into a large volume, perhaps several, by the addition of illustrative material drawn from many centuries and many civilizations, but I do not think that such additions would add much to the basic ideas that I wish to put forward. Also, other tasks, in other fields, demand attention. One day, perhaps, when they are discharged, I may return to the questions raised in this short book. I shall always be grateful to the City College and to the Saposnekow endowment, for without this invitation I am sure the book would never have been written. I would like to record my gratitude to Dean Samuel Middlebrook and his colleagues, who made my visit to the City College such a pleasant one.

J. H. P.

Christ's College,
Cambridge

INTRODUCTION

In this book I have tried to draw a sharp distinction between the past and history. Man, from the earliest days of recorded time, has used the past in a variety of ways: to explain the origins and purpose of human life, to sanctify institutions of government, to give validity to class structure, to provide moral example, to vivify his cultural and educational processes, to interpret the future, to invest both the individual human life or a nation's with a sense of destiny. For all societies the past has been a living past, something which has been used day after day, life after life, never-endingly. The more literate and sophisticated the society becomes, the more complex and powerful become the uses to which the past is put.

The sense of the past has usually been linked in human consciousness with a sense of the future. This is as true of Eastern societies as of Western; yet there was a great difference between them. The Chinese certainly saw the future in terms of the past. The fall of dynasties, due to the withdrawal of Heaven's Mandate through misrule, also predicted the rise of others; also, the rise of a dynasty meant Heaven's approval – the prospect, therefore, of power, prosperity, justice and general well-being. But in the Western Christian world the past was linked to the future in a much more dynamic fashion, for the

Christian cosmology stretched over time future as well as time past in an intricate narrative that predicted particular and precise events. The movement of the past in the West was linear, in the East cyclical, though not without a concept of betterment.

Man is full of curiosity and often a very exact observer. So the past which he used either to sustain himself or his societies was never a mere invention. It contained a great deal of what had actually happened to the tribe or nation to which he belonged or even, if he were royal or belonged to a priestly or warrior class, of what had happened to his own ancestors.

And the fascination of the past as well as its usefulness led him to presume facts about it, to discover others, and to establish their veracity – so long as one remembers that truth may be a moral, a theological, or even an aesthetic truth and not merely a factual one. The majority of men and historians for most of recorded time were concerned with far more than what had merely happened.

But the past, used in the way it was, is never history, although parts of it may be historical. History, like science, is an intellectual process. Like science, too, it requires imagination, creativity and empathy as well as observation as accurate as a scholar can make it. History, like science, has grown intellectually out of all recognition with its ancient self in the last three hundred years in Western societies. And probably the growth of both is subtly linked. But from the

Renaissance onwards there has been a growing determination for historians to try and understand what happened, purely in its own terms and not in the service of religion or national destiny, or morality, or the sanctity of institutions; indeed, to try and bring to the human story both the detachment and insight and intellectual comprehension that natural philosophers have brought to their study of the external world. The historian's growing purpose has been to see things as they really were, and from this study to attempt to formulate processes of social change which are acceptable on historical grounds and none other. This to my mind is a Western development. Some scholars whom I admire will disagree, for they feel that I exaggerate the difference between Chinese and Western historiography. I am aware, as far as reading of translations of secondary authorities permits, of the subtlety of Chinese historiography, of its pre-occupation with documentation and its development of concepts of institutional change which, to some extent, broke through the basic historical generalizations of the Mandate of Heaven concept. Obviously, Chinese historians of the T'ang dynasty were infinitely superior to Einhard or Otto of Freising or any other early medieval chronicler, as superior as Chinese sages were in technology or in administration. Be that as it may, their development never broke the final barriers that lead to true history – the attempt to see things as they were, irrespective of what conflict this might create with what the wise ones of one's own society make of the past. The Chinese pursued erudition, but they never developed the critical historiography which is the signal achievement of Western historians over the last two hundred years. They never attempted, let alone succeeded, in treating history as objective understanding.

The critical historical process has helped to weaken the past, for by its very nature it dissolves those simple, structural generalizations by which our forefathers interpreted the purpose of life in historical terms. Doubtless this is why totalitarian societies keep such a firm hand on their historians and permit them no freedom, except in the accumulation of erudition. In such societies history is still a social process, a sanctification, and not a quest for truth. Basically history is destructive, although it would be wrong to think that it is entirely responsible for destroying the sanction that the past has in religion, politics, education and morals nowadays. The present weakness of the past springs from deeper causes, causes that penetrate deep into the nature of industrial society. Industrial society, unlike the commercial, craft and agrarian societies which it replaces, does not need the past. Its intellectual and emotional orientation is towards change rather than conservation, towards exploitation and consumption. The new methods, new processes, new forms of living of scientific and industrial society have no sanction in the past and no roots in it. The past becomes, therefore, a matter of curiosity, of nostalgia, a sentimentality. Of course, vestiges of its strength remain, particularly in religion and politics, which are still in conflict and in crisis within the new advanced industrial societies. On the other hand, in some aspects of life the domination of the past has disappeared almost completely. Until the late nineteenth century art and architecture were dominated by the past, not only in technique but also in themes. Historical painting was considered to be the highest form of art. Public buildings were either Roman, Greek or Gothic, or variations on those basic themes. But here the past has vanished. Occasionally an artist, even Picasso, will turn to an ancient myth, but rarely to the events of history. And one cannot imagine a skyscraper with flying buttresses or Doric columns. The strength of the past in all aspects of life is far, far weaker than it was a generation ago; indeed, few societies have ever had a past in such a galloping dissolution as this. It could be argued, and perhaps should be, that the dissolution is not fast enough, that the weight of the past on many social, educational and political concepts and institutions is itself helping to create crisis, and that the past, even in its death throes, is taking too long to die. Whatever the truth, some of the responsibility for the past's weakness must be the historians', who have so resolutely attacked mythical, religious and political interpretations of the past.

Does it matter? And can history replace the past in social effectiveness? One simple, yet difficult, question. Yes, it matters. There has so far always been a need in human societies to possess a sense of worth and of value. This, of course, may be provided in non-historical ways – by the quality of life that is experienced, by the sense of identification with the aims and purposes of a group or community. Some men and women can derive it from the richness of their own instinctive lives; for many, the will to live is sufficient justification for being alive.[1] The majority of men and women, however, need the dimension of time because they are conscious of it. They realize that they are a part of an historical process that has changed over the centuries; that time for men and women and their societies can never be static, or at least has never been static; that the process of change has accelerated and is accelerating so that they require to know what the nature of this process has been and is. They need an historical past, objective and true.

The past used to dictate what a man should do or believe; this history cannot do, but at least the historian can describe what has happened and what, therefore, it may be imprudent to do. The historian cannot be free from either moral or political judgments any more than the scientist can be, but he can do his best to form both in the light of history, flick-

[1] 'There is a will to live without rejecting anything of life which is the virtue I honour most in this world': Albert Camus.

ering and feeble though it may be. There are human truths to be derived from history, and truths well worth the telling, some large, some small, some general, some technical. Some, if not the most important, of the problems which face society today are not new ones; there are similarities and analogies in the past. Any process which increases man's awareness of himself, that strengthens his chance of controlling himself and his environment, is well worth pursuing. The death of the past does not deny a future for history. Each one of us is an historical being, held in a pattern created by Time, and to be unconscious of our historical selves is fraught with dangers. History, however, is not the past. The past is always a created ideology with a purpose, designed to control individuals, or motivate societies, or inspire classes. Nothing has been so corruptly used as concepts of the past. The future of history and historians is to cleanse the story of mankind from those deceiving visions of a purposeful past. The death of the past can only do good so long as history flourishes. Above all, one hopes that the past will not rise phoenix-like from its own ashes to justify again, as it so often has, the subjection and exploitation of men and women, to torture them with fears, or to stifle them with a sense of their own hopelessness. The past has only served the few; perhaps history may serve the multitude.

I

THE SANCTION OF
THE PAST

FOR as long as we can discern, the past has loomed
ominously about the lives of men, threatening,
demanding and hinting at cataclysm. It has contained
portents and omens, one god or many. Its dark
firmament has glittered with examples, a few bene-
volent, most doom-laden. Embedded in this mass of
belief, which fulfilled, as we shall see, diverse and
necessary social purposes, were bits and pieces of
truth, notices of events which had taken place, names
of men and women who had actually lived. But until
very recent times there was no history as we know it;
little intention in all those who dealt with the past of
searching for what actually happened and, having discovered this, subjecting it to analysis, in order to
discover what controlled, in material terms, the
destinies of men.[1] Even the greatest historians of

[1] Herbert Butterfield, 'Delays and Paradoxes in the Development
of Historiography', in *Studies in International History*, ed. K. Bourne and
D. C. Watt (1967), 1. 'The truth is that in ages which were capable of
profound philosophy, abstruse mathematics, and subtle self-analysis,
historiography could be very backward, and there would prevail an
amazing credulity about the records and stories of bygone times.'

antiquity, Herodotus, Livy, Tacitus, Ssu-ma Chi'en or Ssu-ma Kuang, never disentangled themselves from the past, from its myth or its social use; only perhaps Thucydides grasped the nature of the problem – the need to reconstruct the past as it happened – and decided that the solution, in any large sense, was impossible, and so he devoted himself to contemporary events, events which he could explore through his own senses before Time had eroded or destroyed the evidence.[1] But even the contemporary history of Thucydides, governed as it was by a precise and exacting mind, was not history in our sense. Thucydides was pursuing truths, not historical truth, but truths about men's behaviour in war and politics – the nature of man, the operation of chance, courage and weakness, good and evil – and therefore he permitted himself imaginative methods, such as his opposed dialogues, which are as alien to history as we know it as alchemy is to the scientist.

The same is also true of the greatest historian of Classical China, Ssu-ma Chi'en. *The Memoirs of an Historian* was probably started by his father, Ssu-ma Tan, the Grand Astrologer, but most of it was written

[1] For Thucydides, see the perceptive remarks by M. I. Finley, *The Greek Historians* (1959), 7–14: 'The paradox is that to give meaning to history he [Thucydides] tended to abandon history.' Also A. Momigliano, 'Time in Ancient Historiography', *History and Theory* (Wesleyan University Press, Middletown, 1966), Beiheft 6, 11–12, and M. I. Finley, 'Myth, Memory and History', *History and Theory* (1964–65), iv, 299.

by the son, who succeeded him in his office and completed it in the gloomiest circumstances (towards the end of his life he was castrated for attempting to deceive the throne). It is a remarkable, but odd, achievement. Most of it is compilatory. Ssu-Ma Chi'en copied out those archaic texts which he could discover, modernizing the language somewhat but largely accepting what he was told. Legends and truth are intermingled, particularly in the biographies of dukes, officials, sages and bandits which form so large a part of his work. Nevertheless, at times Ssu-ma Chi'en demonstrates a sophisticated awareness of the difficulty of arriving at historic truth. On the other hand he accepts the records of the most improbable and detailed conversations without the slightest expression of doubt. These are in the accepted record, so down they go into his. The whole effect, however, of this remarkable book, which contains, as well as annals and biographies, treatises on music, astrology, irrigation, rites, sacrifices and the calendar, is quite unlike what we regard as history. In many ways it is a handbook for bureaucrats, telling them of the past. Ssu-ma Chi'en's book conveys large quantities of information to demonstrate the interplay between the aspirations of moral life and the course of reality. There is no historical *criticism* as we know it – no attempt to understand the past as a time different from our own. Ssu-ma Chi'en is concerned to demonstrate what happens when men depart from the dictates of Heaven and the rules of morality by examples from the past. He wished to show how even the emperors themselves could lose the Mandate of Heaven by not ruling according to the principles of Confucius. The past for him was a moral guide, the example of the higher truths, an illustration of principles, not a matter for analysis. And the records and events which he wished to preserve were illustrations for which their position in time, their chronological context, was not of prime significance. His book, vast and valuable as it is, is more a narrative of morality than a narrative of history.[1]

And when we come to Livy or to Tacitus, the same element is dominant. History is to teach, and its imaginative and moral truths are more important than factual accuracy or original documentation. Of course, neither Livy nor Tacitus despised exactitude, particularly Tacitus, but their concern was with private virtue and public morality. Their aim was to illustrate the qualities which had led Rome to her greatness and to investigate the weaknesses which often caused her to be less than herself. The great

[1] For Ssu-ma Chi'en, see C. P. Fitzgerald, *China* (3rd ed., 1961), 208–17; E. Chavannes, *Les Mémoires Historiques de Se-ma Ts'ien* (5 vols., Paris, 1895–1905); *The Records of the Grand Historian of China*, trans. Burton Watson (2 vols., New York, 1961); Burton Watson, *Ssu-ma Chi'en, Grand Historian of China* (New York, 1958), particularly chaps. iii, iv and v; A. F. P. Hulsewé, 'Notes on the Historiography of the Han Period', in *Historical Writing on the Peoples of Asia: Historians of China and Japan*, ed. W. G. Beasley and E. G. Pulleyblank (Oxford, 1961).

writers of antiquity were using the material of past times in order to explore their own problems about the moral qualities of men or society. More than this, implicit in their work is the fateful intervention of supernatural forces, which is particularly strong in Herodotus and Livy, even though less so in Thucydides and Tacitus. These are usually connected with the intervention of the gods in human life.[1] Man must reckon with them, though it is uncertain whether man can really avoid what is ordained. Furthermore, the gods may be capricious. And the same is not only true for the sophisticated historians of China, for whom history confirms what disasters befall dynasties of the Sons of Heaven when they depart from its dictates, but also for the epic bards of the primitive

[1] In Chinese history, the gods are infinitely remote; the activating principle of the Mandate of Heaven is ethical and eternal. The Chinese use of the past developed along the lines laid down by Ssuma Chi'en, although it became for a time much more limited in scope. Committees of historians wrote the history of the previous dynasty as factually as they could, but of course indicating the ways in which the Sons of Heaven lost their mandate and the new dynasty of emperors gained theirs. The cramping nature of this method was realized by later Chinese historians, who were aware of the need to trace institutional development irrespective of dynastic change. In consequence, their writing became ever more sophisticated within the terms of their intention, but their intention remained moral and educative, as the title of the great work of the finest historian of them all, Ssu-ma Kuang demonstrates – *Comprehensive Mirror for Aid in Government*, the title bestowed on it by the Sung Emporer, Shen-tsung. Until modern times this terse, explanatory title would have been appropriate for much Western as well as Eastern history.

Vikings. Their sagas, in which gods and demons slip in and out of the lives of historical figures, are clouded with a sense of tragic fate, of the hopelessness and helplessness of men caught in time. The past is a psychological reality, used for a social purpose to stress the virtues of courage, endurance, strength, loyalty and indifference to death. The sagas are, in fact, the living past, not history, even if the core of events is derived from actuality. Burnt Njal and Aud the Deep-Minded may have been historical personages, but that was an indifferent matter to the saga-makers. What counted for them was the doom-haunted, blood-dripping story of their lives which conveyed the deepest sense of truth to those tiny isolated bands of seafarers and farmers in the lonely valleys of Iceland and by the desolate shores of Greenland. For them the past had to be as real, as living, as the ghost-haunted wind; as certain as the power of the stars. And for a past that lives, what is time? – an irrelevance; as generation followed generation, Grettir, like Odysseus, fulfilled a human and social need, illuminated men's nature and made propaganda for the virtues that society required. And the past in the Greek world was just as much a living entity, a social necessity, as amongst the Norsemen or Saxons. 'Annually the mythical heroes reappeared at the great religious festivals in tragedy and choral ode, and they recreated for their audiences the unbroken web of all life, stretching back over generations of men to the gods...all this was serious and true, literally true.'[1]

When history is indissolubly entangled in myth and legend, its value is personal as well as social. The Greek audience, listening at a street corner to Herodotus reciting a part of his work,[2] or sitting through the tragedies of Sophocles, or the Festival of Dionysus, was accepting as truth these interpretations of human destiny and the nature of the gods. They were seeking, as men have since they first became conscious of their own status, the meaning of Time when related to themselves, with its harsh facts of birth, growth and death. And this, not curiosity, is man's first and primary involvement with the past, the deep emotional basis for his preoccupation with legend, with myth, with heroes, with gods, whether they all be monstrous or benign. It lies at the root of all preoccupations with the past – Chinese, Greek, Egyptian, Norse, Vedic and Judaic. And as might be expected, the answers that were given to the common man were as mysterious as the oracles of Delphi, yet always charged with his fears and hopes. Wherever one looks in these early societies, one is struck by the doom-ridden nature of the past which men constructed for themselves. Njal is burnt alive; Grettir's salt-embalmed head is tossed at his mother's feet. Oedipus is blinded. Prometheus is tortured for eternity. Adam and Eve were cast out of Eden; Abel slaughtered by his

---

[1] Finley, 'Myth, Memory and History', loc. cit. 283.
[2] Anthony Andrewes, *The Greeks* (1967), 264.

brother Cain. Men knew that disaster befell the innocent or that tragedy overtook the generous-hearted.[1] Not that it was all chance, tribulation and wantonness; after all, just retribution came to Thorbjörn Angle, Grettir's killer: his head was sliced in half by Grettir's brother, who, though adulterous, also secured a rich and beautiful Byzantine noblewoman. Absolved by the Church, he died in the odour of sanctity. Evil met its doom, reward came to the just, though peccant. And some myths are joyful, many hopeful. The past becomes the theatre of life.

And, of course, the past was deeply embedded in all religions which attempted to give systematic answers to man's concern with birth, death and the endless progression of the generations. Furthermore, an explanation of the past, or its use in ritual, whether it be baptism or sacrifice to ancestors, was essential for social stability, and therefore an essential part of government. No early governments could hope to rule without the active use of the past; hence the need for state religion in the earliest days of Egypt or Sumer. Most religions attempted to domesticate Time through what they believed to be the nature of the past in order to reconcile the mass of mankind to

[1] Here there is a difference, and an important one, between China and other societies. History, even the earliest in China, is concerned with dynasties, and the disfavour of Heaven was always due to the weakness, selfishness and immorality of men. There is very little sense of personal doom and capricious gods in early Chinese historical literature.

the heavy burden of agrarian life. The past was important in descending orders of society – to kings, emperors, Pharaohs, tyrants, consuls or tribunes, high priests. For these classes of men it was, and for most of the generations of recorded history has been, of exceptional importance. But for peasants, for the worker in the field, or for the craftsman toiling in his slum, these were concerned only with the immediate past, with their own ancestors, their own gods, with whom they often lived in the closest proximity. Time, for them, concerned their own mortality.

The ruling class, however, used the past for other purposes than to explain man's complex destiny, to reconcile him to his condition, to lead him to accept the inevitable process of Time or to teach him how he might overcome death by the examples of the past.[1] All rulers needed an interpretation of the past to justify the authority of their government, and often the priests and officials required explanations that would reconcile changes of dynasty or periods of defeat to the general pattern of interpretation which their society had developed. As we have noted, the Chinese sages and historians explained the rise and fall of dynasties by the idea of the withdrawal of Heaven's Mandate. And so their past provided

[1] This is particularly true of the Egyptians' view of the past in the Book of the Dead, in which the dead person is identified with the god (Osiris) who has in the past overcome death: S. G. F. Brandon, *History, Time and Deity* (Manchester, 1965), 22–23, 78–79.

example after example of men of modest birth who, aided by virtue and skill, secured Heaven's Mandate and became the Son of Heaven, the priest-king of the Chinese Empire. When their descendants, however, less wise and more indulgent, departed from a proper reverence for their ancestor's example, they lost the support of Heaven. Inevitably their dynasty crumbled and was replaced. Once the sign of Heaven was clear, there was nothing disloyal, nothing treasonable in giving devotion to the new emperor, for he was blessed by the ancestral spirits of China. This gave a sense of moral continuity to a throne that was continually fought for both by the Chinese and by Mogul invaders. It even allowed for acceptance of periods of political anarchy, which might have to be endured until the Mandate of Heaven became clear. Around this concept there gradually accrued a huge body of accurate historical observation – of famines, floods, economic decline, etc., which could be used as proof of the primary concept. The Chinese sages used the past in more sophisticated ways than this to give a sense of order and perpetuity to their world. The past in their society had a constant daily social purpose. Nevertheless, the essence of its use lay in the concept of the Mandate of Heaven – to secure social subjection and continuity in a world of political change.

This use of the past for social purposes occurs in all early civilizations for which we have written records. In them the past legitimizes authority and status. This

is the reason for the primitive king-lists which are
some of the earliest historical records of human
society. The Palermo Stone (probably of about
2500 B.C.) took the Pharaohs back to pre-dynastic
times, recalling the events for which they were
famous; recorded with equal care was the yearly
height of the Nile's inundation.[1] This, of course,
was not a piece of ancient antiquarianism, nor created
to satisfy intellectual curiosity. It was designed to
perpetuate the sense of endless continuity of kingship, right back to the gods themselves, and to assoc-
iate in the same long corridor of the past the most
vital event of Egyptian life – the flooding of the
waters. Similarly, the famous genealogy of the
Memphite priests, which lists sixty generations from
c. 750 B.C. back to c. 2100, descending in an unbroken
succession of fathers and sons, fulfils the same purpose.[2] It uses the overwhelming authority of the past

[1] *The Idea of History in the Ancient Near East*, ed. Robert C. Dentan
(Yale University Press, New Haven, 1955), 6 ff., for a discussion by
Ludlow Bull of other Egyptian king-lists.

[2] Brandon, *History, Time and Deity*, 66 ff. In his eagerness to refute
Professor Eliade's theory of *L'Eternel Retour*, Brandon fails to discuss
the social purpose of these monuments and, I think, attributes to the
Egyptians an antiquarianism which is probably anachronistic. The
archaism in art which may be discernible in the Saite period (663–525
B.C.) can be related to the same social purpose as the king-lists to enhance the authority of the present by linking it visibly with the
grandeur of the past. For the same reasons English gentlemen in the
eighteenth century built palaces which they called Palladian and
referred to themselves as Augustans. Whatever is built for the working class, however, is usually strictly contemporary.

to enhance the status of those who possess the genealogy. The same process was at work amongst the
Hebrews; think of those endless lists of everlasting
begats that fill the early chapters of the Book of
Chronicles, so that distant relationship with the
patriarchs could be established. Such relationships
contained charisma, they sanctioned the authority
and status of those who could claim the historic
heritage. The Sumer king-lists were similarly designed to link kings with gods through time, a habit
still current amongst the aristocracy of Plato's Athens.
In a similar way the feudal aristocracy in ancient
China appropriated the past, changing a primitive
fertility religion into ancestor worship from whose
rites the peasants were rigorously excluded.[1] Workers
and ancestors do not mix; they never have. Myth,
usually terrifying, provides for the worker; the official
past is the property of government.

This acquisition of the past by the ruling and
possessing classes and the exclusion of the mass of the
peasantry and labouring class is a widespread phenomenon through recorded time.[2] The authoritarian

[1] Fitzgerald, *China*, 44–45: 'In ancient and feudal times ancestor
worship was the cult of the noble clans. The peasantry, separated in
their way of life and in their marriage customs from the aristocracy,
had no part in it.'

[2] 'Genealogy was the most personal and abiding concern of the
great mid-twelfth-century Saxon historian known as Annalista
Saxo': K. Leyser, 'The German Aristocracy in the Early Middle Ages',
Past and Present, no. 41 (Dec. 1968), 52. In this fascinating and perceptive article, Leyser points out that the writers of the tenth and

purposes of genealogy for society have not been much emphasized by historians. Nor has this use of the past been limited to antiquity. The chroniclers of the Tudor monarchy, Fabyan, Hall, Holinshed, Baker and the rest, were just as eager to trace the unbroken succession of their monarchs as any Sumerian. These Tudor historians drew a quick and certain line back to the Conquest, to Alfred, to the mythical Lud, but did not stop there; on they went back to David and the House of Jesse, right back to Adam himself. These genealogies are no different in social purpose from Sumerian king-lists or the lists in the Book of Chronicles.

Nor is it merely kings and Pharaohs or high priests who have required the authority of an ancestral table. All aristocracies have, very sensibly, made a cult of genealogy in order to underpin their special status. And it is interesting, if not surprising, that outbreaks of genealogical fever occur most frequently when new classes are emerging into status, a new faction pushing its way into the ancient aristocracy, or when

---

eleventh centuries, drawn from the monasteries, cathedrals and the courts, were preoccupied with the nobility and there was scarcely any mention of any other class. 'The assumption was that nobility had merit and merit again was innate in blood': ibid. 27. Hence monastic chroniclers revelled in the royal, princely, ducal or merely noble founders of their houses in the same way that Homer had related his heroes to the gods or the saga writers theirs to the dwellers in Valhalla. The personal ownership of the past has always been a vital strand in the ideology of all ruling classes.

the established ruling classes feel threatened by the *nouveaux riches*. When, as happened in England between 1550 and 1650, all of these three factors were present at the same time, the effect on the cult of genealogy was dramatic.[1] '. . . as early as 1577 Walter, Earl of Essex was boasting of his fifty-five quarterings, so England was clearly already well set on the road to the heraldic fantasy world whose finest hour came at the end of the eighteenth century with the 719 quarterings of the Grenvilles depicted on the ceiling of their Gothic Library at Stowe.'[2] Where the service of the past has been urgently need-ed, truth has ever been at a discount. As most of the Elizabethan aristocracy's true genealogies tended to disappear after a generation or so either into oblivion or, even worse, into a yeoman's family, they forged

[1] See Michael Maclagen, 'Genealogy and Heraldry in the Sixteenth and Seventeenth Centuries', in *English Historical Scholarship in the Sixteenth and Seventeenth Centuries,* ed. Levi Fox (Oxford, 1956), 31–48; G. D. Squibb, *The High Court of Chivalry* (Oxford, 1959). The College of Arms was granted a new charter in 1555 by Mary I, and the acquisition of arms by the gentry changed from a canter to a gallop. Forgeries of genealogies and arms were common. A notorious provider, William Dawkyns, who lost his ear in 1577 for corrupt heraldic practices, was charged twenty years later with similar offen-ces. Noblemen as well as mere gentry grew idolatrous about their ancestral past. The Dormers erected a splendid monument dis-playing their arms, twenty-four shields in all; eight of them were probably invented for this monument, as not a trace of them exists previously.

[2] Lawrence Stone, *The Crisis of the Aristocracy, 1558–1641* (1965), 25.

medieval charters, cut ancient seals and invented ancestors with panache. Lord Burghley, the scion of a modest Welsh family, got himself back to Edward the Confessor's day; others were less modest and claimed Charlemagne, Roman consuls and even Trojans. Not to be outdone, the Pophams indiscreetly placed an ark in their family tree.[1] But this was no joke, no game, no fantasy; both arms and pedigrees were of vital use. The great painted genealogies had a purpose every whit as definitive as the great stele of Sethy I at Abydos where he is depicted venerating the names of his seventy-six predecessors (naturally pruned, of course, of such heretics as Aknen-Atun and his followers or of the successful invaders, the Hyksos). So has the power descended, so is power confirmed.[2] As it was for Sethy I, so it had to be for the first Lord Burghley, and so it was to be, but in how diminished a sense, for many New Englanders caught up in the genealogical craze which

[1] Ibid. 23. Maclagen, op. cit. 38. See also Sir Anthony Wagner, *English Genealogy* (Oxford, 1960); F. Smith Fussner, *The Historical Revolution* (1962), 42–44. The formidable J. H. Round permitted himself a field day of mockery in his *Family Origins and Other Studies*, ed. W. Page (1930), but he missed the powerful social drives which made this emblematic personalization of the past an essential human, and class, need. Normans, Saxons, Romans or Trojans were as essential to the Elizabethans as Priam, Hector or Achilles to the Greeks; just as Gaul and Charlemagne were to the aristocracy at the court of Louis XIV.

[2] Dentan (ed.), *The Idea of History in the Ancient Near East*, 8. An illustration of the bas-relief is to be found in Brandon, *History, Time and Deity*, plate x.

swept America in the 1880s and 1890s.[1] The newly arrived Americans, daunted by the Winthrops, the Cabots and lesser families who could trace their pedigrees to the Pilgrim Fathers and beyond, required a personal share of the past to bolster their new-found social status and authority. Alas, there was no American College of Arms to provide their wants, no Garter King-of-Arms to bribe, no Bluemantle to suborn, but the New York Public Library did its best, acquired the largest of all genealogical departments; so-called genealogists worked, with about the same sense of historical accuracy as their Tudor predecessors, in the major record offices of Europe. The Scottish clans were revitalized, the tartan industry launched, and ancestor worship, if pale by Chinese standards, acquired a certain respectability. But like so many uses of the past that reach back to the dawn of time, the force of genealogy withered, and what was once an essential need for social and political authority became the plaything of snobbery or of mere nationalist obsessions.[2] This is the first

[1] J. H. Plumb, 'The Historians' Dilemma', in *The Crisis in the Humanities*, ed. J. H. Plumb (1964), 40.

[2] There is one aspect of genealogy, however, which paradoxically reverses the historical process: instead of the past confirming honour and authority on the present, the Mormons search for genealogical truth in order to confer honour on the dead by retrospective baptism. Nowhere is geneaology more powerful than in Salt Lake City, where family records are preserved with the same care that was lavished on the mummies of the Pharaohs. The records are buried deep in rock caverns, nuclear-bomb proof.

instance, but it will not be the last, of the decay of the past, of old forces losing their personal and social content. If genealogy may be active and useful as a professional technique[1] and a harmless pastime for the snob and the antiquarian, it has lost its authority for society – so much so that we underestimate its force, not only in early societies, but also in recent times.[2] Men did not emblazon their houses, their coaches, their tombs, for mere whimsy, nor paint elaborate pedigrees on their walls or spend good money to have them forged for mere personal ostentation and satisfaction. The credulous mass needed to be impressed by these outward emblems of antique status. Their possessors had been blessed in their authority by Time itself.

If king-lists, genealogies and the like are as old as recorded history, as old as the first stories of Creation, or of those mythical times of gods and men and heroes which for all societies was the living past against

[1] It has proved of exceptional value in the latest developments in demography which began with the publication of *Le Beauvais et le Beauvaisis de 1600 à 1730*, by Pierre Goubert (2 vols., Paris, 1960). See also 'Daedalus', *Journal of the American Academy of Arts and Science*, vol. 97, no. 2 (1968).

[2] Genealogy may have been given additional strength and plausibility by the fact that Time was limited. The Creation was not far away, namely in 4004 B.C. Popular middle-class attacks on the folly of genealogy start up in the nineteenth century. 'This whole claim of Norman descent for a few families is a frivolous pride . . . for seeing that even twenty generations back every person must have 1,300,896 great, great, great, etc. grandfathers and grandmothers.' Rev. F. W. Farrar, *The People of England* (n.d.), 35.

which their lives were lived, so too are annals. Although descent from the gods obviously confirmed status and authority on kings and aristocrats and priests, it was insufficient for any complex state based on authoritarian kingship and bent on expansion of its territory and power. Struggles for power between states are discernible in the very dawn of recorded time, between the lower and upper parts of Egypt, between Ur and Lagash in the delta of the Euphrates, between Shang and Chou in the great basin of the Yellow River. In such circumstances, dynasties were overturned, the power of cities rose and fell, and with the rise and fall of dynasties and cities so the gods, too, changed their status. Families of priests and noblemen, blessed with family trees as old as the Creation, were obliterated. The wheel of fortune spun wildly; it needed explanation unless authority was to seem capricious. The past was like an elaborate house of cards which the present was constantly upsetting. But power needs legitimacy, and when not based on consent, when it is absolutist or oligarchic, it needs justification, which it can get in three ways: from religion, from philosophy, from the past – and, of course, more often than not, it uses an amalgam of the three.

Some societies solved the problem easily. The Sumerians, Akkadians and Assyrians denied immortality of the soul; immortality was reserved for the gods, so all disasters, all perturbations of state could be explained as the result of a theological offence.[1] But even so, their chroniclers had some problems. Marduck, the god of Babylon, was far from being the highest god of the Pantheon, yet Babylon triumphed over all cities. This, too, was solved with that persuasive simplicity which the Babylonians brought to fundamental problems. No god was omnipotent. They could fight and defeat one another, even though they could not kill one another. So the rise and fall of the cities of which they were the deities reflected their heavenly combat. Yet even so, the relations between kings and gods were very complex. Kings must not commit, or even seem to commit, a theological offence. And the god of the city, or of the chief city, had to be precisely aware of this. It was vitally important for a king, therefore, to keep an ancient covenant with the gods that might have been made by his predecessors. It was equally important that the gods should be informed about the actions of kings so that there could be no mistake about intention. Hence the need for chronicles, for annals, or for the letters of Assyrian kings to their gods. The past was constantly involved in the present, and all that enshrined the past, monuments, inscriptions, records, were essential weapons in government, in securing

---

[1] 'This motif of theological offence as grounds for historic change confronts us throughout Mesopotamian history': E. A. Speiser, 'Ancient Mesopotamia', in Dentan (ed.), *The Idea of History in the Ancient Near East*, 57.

the authority, not only of the king, but also of those whose power he symbolized and sanctified. The purpose, the maintenance of authority, was simple, not complex, and it moulded the explanation: defeat was the scourge due to a god's neglect; failure to attend to a god's wants could lead him to turn his back on his people as the god Nidoba had done on his city of Lagash. In such a world the defeated were always wicked and the successful righteous. The past cannot be more simply used than this, yet its simplicity has never hurt its popularity. The same historical methods, hoary with age, were used by Cyrus, in 539 B.C., when Babylon's turn came. Yet primitive as this type of method may be in handling the past, it was, in various forms, to last not only for centuries but millennia. Annalistic history, until very recent times, has been, with hagiography and biography, the dominant method of dealing with the past. It is true that the activities of the gods have been pushed further and further into the background, but the general purpose of annals, whether they be written by Livy, by Tacitus, by the ancient Chinese sages, or by Baker, Holinshed or Fabyan, or Macaulay, Bancroft or Bishop Stubbs, have the same fundamental purpose: to explain the past in order to strengthen and to serve the authority of the ruling powers. Disasters, setbacks, even defeats, conspiracies and rebellions, can be contemplated so long as the result is right. But obviously, as societies become more complex, more sophisticated in their traditions, and more varied in their class structure, and more diverse become the sources of social and political power, so does the problem posed *to* the annalist become more difficult to solve, calling on greater powers, not so much of historical analysis as of literary ingenuity. The differences between the *Annals* and *Histories* of Tacitus and the Book of Chronicles are at first sight staggering; the highly sophisticated contrasts sharply with the simple. Yet the purpose of both is the same. As Hugh Lloyd-Jones has reminded us, 'All ancient history – perhaps all history – is the history of a ruling oligarchy.'[1] But it is more than this; it always contains, as indeed the *Annals* and *Histories* of Tacitus do, a justification of the authority of the state. History as criticism of the basis of power and authority, rather than history as criticism of the way men may have used it, is of very recent origin in the history of human society. This method of dealing with the past by narration of events of particular peoples, nations or communities in order to justify authority, to create confidence and to secure stability, opens up a huge complex

[1] *Tacitus, the Annals and the Histories,* ed. and abridged by Hugh Lloyd-Jones (1966), xxxviii. Daniel Hensius expressed similar thoughts in the early seventeenth century: 'If history have no professorship, if all universities be closed, she will always have an honourable reception in palaces, and in the innermost chambers of Kings and princes', quoted from *The Value of History,* trans. G. W. Robinson (Cambridge, Mass., 1943), by Donald R. Kelley, 'Historia Integra: François Baudouin and his Conception of History', *Journal of the History of Ideas,* xxv (1964), 35-39.

of ideas that is far too vast to deal with here in the detail which it deserves. And I only wish, at this point, to emphasize one aspect of it. I have used the example of Ancient Mesopotamia because of its simplicity, because, like the cleaned skeleton of an animal or bird, it displays the obvious. But every literate society which has so far existed has needed to use the past for the same fundamental purpose. The past has always been the handmaid of authority.

It is not accidental that great social crises, when secular authority or ancient beliefs are torn in conflict, bring forth a huge spate of historical writing and, indeed, historical controversy. Warring authorities mean warring pasts. The same is true when ecclesiastical as well as political power is the battleground. Consider the great output of historical literature in the third and fourth centuries, when Christianity was at last supplanting paganism as the religion of the state – an upheaval of stupendous proportions which changed fundamentally a cultural climate which had lasted for nearly a millennium.[1] Again, the Reformation and Counter-Reformation produced a rapid increase in historical writing and discussion; indeed, it was at this point that history for the first time became recognized as a minority discipline.[2] And for

[1] *The Conflict between Paganism and Christianity in the Fourth Century* (Oxford, 1963), ed. A. Momigliano, 79–99.

[2] Kelley, op. cit. 39–40: 'In Protestant Germany history made even more substantial gains. As a result especially of Melanchthon's educational reforms some universities began to provide for *professores*

a more local example, the political strife of the seventeenth century in England plunged almost the entire governing class into historical studies.[1] Although both periods were exceptionally seminal, as we shall see, for the growth of true history, the resolution of these conflicts brought a diminution in historical activity and the acceptance of an historical orthodoxy, whether it be St Augustine on the one hand or the Whig interpretation of English history on the other. During such a time of conflict, the past has to be fought for as well as the present. Authority, once achieved, must have a secure and usable past. At least, this has been true until very recent times. Yet, as with genealogy and chronology, the need seems to be passing, although the reasons for the failure of this type of history may be subtler; but there is no doubt that its hold is weakening.[2] And for the first time in this book, I toll the bell for the past which is dying. One has only to consider the fate of the Whig inter-

---

historianium so that history achieved parity not only with poetry but even, according to some pedagogical schemes, with law and theology.'

[1] J. G. A. Pocock, *The Ancient Constitution and the Feudal Law* (Cambridge, 1957).

[2] The multi-volume narrative history of a particular country or of an epoch in its history was very widely practised in the nineteenth century; indeed, it became the most popular of all forms of history and established the reputation of such giants as Michelet, Thiers, Ranke, Macaulay, Stubbs, Gardiner, Klyuchevsky, Bancroft, Henry Adams, to name but a few. However, at the turn of the century narrative history entered upon a sharp decline and it is no longer practised on the grand scale by professional historians. There has also

pretation of history in England, the decline of which is due not only to the attacks to which it has been subjected by technical history,[1] but also because it no longer fills the social needs of an oligarchy of declining power. True, it is still to be found. Its most unashamed exponents are the deeply assertive, popular historians such as Sir Arthur Bryant, whose most recent work, entitled *The Protestant Island*, might have been written for the Victorian public school.[2] But for the new scientists and technologists, the men who man or run nuclear power stations and computer services, this so-called past of their society can at best be no more than nostalgic. It can have no social validity; it cannot give them a sense of purpose. It cannot provide a framework to their authority or a justification for it, as it did not only to a Macaulay in India, but also to scores of minor civil servants there. For such men their past was as meaningful as their religion. And the same is true of France. In spite of

been a similar decline in multi-volume biography. The demand for such histories has died too. See the very perceptive remarks of Richard Hofstadter on the influence of Frederick Jackson Turner on this development in American historiography, in *The Progressive Historians* (New York, 1968), 73. It was, however, a general phenomenon in historical writing.

[1] The fusillade started with the publication by Herbert Butterfield of his *Whig Interpretation of History* in 1931, a most appropriate date, for this year, more than any other, proclaimed the coming dissolution of the British Empire. After that opening shot, bombardment came thick and fast and still continues.

[2] A. Bryant, *The Protestant Island* (1967).

de Gaulle's concern with the past glories of France, the days of Michelet are over. Gone, too, is the Napoleonic legend and with it the belief that France's revolutionary past gave her a special authority on matters of liberty and equality. After the paranoia and disaster of Hitler, the Germanic past – the past of the *Aufklärung* and of Hegel – possesses no hope, nor sense of affirmation, but only of nightmare. Although there is still much history in America that is as affirmatory as it is annalistic, the situation, even there, is becoming immensely schizophrenic. That image of the past – perhaps one should call it the American image – of America as the land of opportunity, of equality of men before God, of liberty and personal freedom, hardly buoys up the establishment in the face of both Negro riots and the war in Vietnam. On the other hand there are aspects of the American past, very appropriate to the present, but no longer usable. The steady expansion of American imperialism through war and finance which led to territorial expansion at the expense of Mexico, of Spain, and to the economic subjection of much of Latin America has never been clothed in an ideology acceptable to the American governing classes as a whole.[1] The concept of Manifest Destiny did its best to confirm war, expansion and suppression, but it never captured so much of the American imagination as a similar

[1] See Robert L. Beisner, *Twelve Against Empire: The Anti-Imperialists, 1898-1900* (New York, 1968).

process did in Britain, whose governing class was able to use the imperialist past in the nineteenth and early twentieth centuries. The use of the past in this way, that is, the confirmatory annals that justify not only the structure of society but its rulers, may not be dead, but it is mortally sick – at least in the West. There is little sense in any Western nation that their past is impelling them towards a certain future. For them, if not for Marxist nations, the concept of Manifest Destiny is stricken, a threadbare refuge for politicians, for ageing rulers of society, but from which all strong social emotion is rapidly draining away.

However, as one might expect when the past has become institutionalized, it remains strong. In the institutions of government, whether they be a presidency or a monarchy, a congress or a parliament, tradition and precedent still possess force. The governing classes of modern society still need their pasts, though not perhaps quite so desperately as the Pharaohs needed their king-lists. But even here tradition, precedent and custom are far, far weaker than they were a generation ago. Government is controlled more by the present than by the past, indeed almost more by the future. The same is even true of law. Case histories and precedents still play their part, but the concept that customary law has a peculiar virtue of its own is now rarely held. Even the Churches, the institutions in which the past plays so dominant and so sacred a role, are paying far less attention to ancient attitudes. The Archbishop of Canterbury embraces the Pope of Rome; Methodists communicate in St Paul's Cathedral. The rack and the anathema are put away. The sanctions of the past for ecclesiastical government and behaviour are losing their efficacy. Naturally, in the institutions of government and of belief, inertia is greater than in social custom and behaviour, but nevertheless it is obvious that even in these ancient citadels the past is weakening. Breaches have been made in the walls, and it no longer sanctions law or belief in the way that it did a generation ago.

The past, however, not only justified, it educated. It had to contain the wisdom, the morality, the dreams and the solace. It was needed to strengthen the purpose of those who possessed power and, equally important, to reconcile those who lacked it. All who were literate turned to it, at some time or other, not only for knowledge, but for human truths. Hence there grew up from the earliest times a wisdom literature which used the past for its material. Not only is this wisdom literature positive, it is also negative; it provides for the cynic, the solitary, the defeated, the sensualist, as well as for the ruler, the conqueror, the bureaucrat and the believer.

> What are their places (now)?
> Their walls are broken apart: and their places are not—
> As though they had never been!
> There is none who comes back from (over) there,
> That he may tell their state,

That he may tell their needs
That he may still our hearts.

or

Since the days of yore there has been no
     permanence;
The resting and the dead, how alike they are!
Do they not compose a picture of death
The commoner and the noble
Once they are near to their fate.

or

Ascend thou into the ruins of cities, go to those
     of old,
Behold the skulls of the latter and the former
     ones.
Which is now an evil-doer, which now a
     benefactor?

The first poem is from the Egyptian *Song of the
Harper,* written possibly about 2000 B.C. the second
is from the *Epic of Gilgamesh,* the earliest of Sumerian
poems, the third from an Assyrian text of the eighth
century B.C.[1] And if we went on down the centuries
or moved to the great civilizations of the East, we
should find, over and over again, the same highly
literate, highly sophisticated attitude to the past – that
all it can teach us is that all is vanity, that there is
nothing new and therefore *carpe diem,* gather rose-
buds, but do not question, do not criticize, accept the

[1] These quotations are all taken from Brandon, *History, Time and
Deity,* 79–82.

THE SANCTION OF THE PAST

wretched fate of man which is written in the annals of time. This is the past, and we shall meet it again in less obvious contexts, as the anodyne, the opium, not of the masses, but of the sensitive intellectual, of men who have never competed for power, or withdrawn from it, or failed in its pursuit.[1]

[1] This is particularly true of Chinese poetry.

> Wandering to and fro amidst the hills and mounds
> Everywhere around us we see dwellings of ancient men.
> Here are vestiges of their wells and hearthstones,
> There the rotted stumps of bamboo and mulberry groves.
> I stop and ask a faggot-gatherer:
> 'These men – what has become of them?'

> . . . .

> In the same world men lead different lives;
> Some at the court, some in the marketplace.
> Indeed I know these are no empty words:
> The life of man is like a shadow-play
> Which must in the end return to nothingness.

T'ao Chi'en (365–427), trans. William Acker, *Anthology of Chinese Literature*, ed. Cyril Birch (1967), 202. Or see *The Ruins of Lo-Yang* by Wei Wen-ti (188–227) in Arthur Waley, *170 Chinese Poems* (1928), 60, and the fascinating fragment of an Anglo-Saxon poem with which Waley links it in sentiment with its splendid last two lines:

> Earth's grip haveth
> Wealders and workmen.

See also C. J. Chi'ên and Michael Bullock, *Poems of Solitude* (1960), particularly 'The Ruined City'.

No governing class has ever been able to provide a life of power, action and authority for all of its members even had they been temperamentally suited for such pursuits, which, of course, some were not. Hence there has always been a need for a philosophy of withdrawal, of the cultivation of the personality in its highest sense,

At times the past becomes nostalgic for more than individuals. There are shifts of power from time to time in the governing class of any nation, and those who lose tend to romanticize the past in order to compensate themselves for what they no longer enjoy, often at the same time denouncing the decadence, the corruption of the times in which they have to live. Two examples must suffice. In England in the late seventeenth and early eighteenth centuries, power shifted from an hierarchical society of self-conscious status to a more open world of the great entrepreneurs, capitalists, bankers and overseas merchants; in consequence there developed amongst the losers a keen sense of nostalgia which romanticized an England in which honour and status were revered more than power and money. It was an attitude that persisted for generations. Similarly in New England, the hatred amongst its Brahmins of immigration, industrialization and democratization resulted in a cult of the primitive colonial period – of the upright-

---

particularly so as many of the useless, the unlucky or the rejected tend to be men of intelligence and sensitivity. For such groups the past as a comment on the illusions of the present has always had a powerful appeal. In all oligarchical societies there is a sensitive and moving poetry in which the past is used as a comment on human vanity. It is to some extent the emotional counterpart to the working classes' religious primitivism, which compensates for their present deprivation with a heavenly future. In China, where there was a large literate bureaucratic class often ruined or exiled by the whims of their ruler, the need for such an attitude was very powerful.

ness, honesty, thrift, frugality and rugged individuality of the early settlers of New England; again a past of nostalgia. The past has often been used as compensation, as a dream time for classes of men as well as individuals; indeed, sometimes nations found solace in the past, particularly small nations absorbed by larger – the romantic cult in Scotland, with its idealization of the clans and of Bonnie Prince Charlie, is a case in point.[1]

This negative attitude to the past has always been the cult of a minority – of the sensitive, the rejected, the retired, or of a section of the governing class that may be losing power. The majority, the active, purposeful part of the governing class and its supporters, required the past to inculcate virtue, to help to create the ideas and attitudes which the state might need and above all to provide human models of virtue. The historical exemplar is legion, from the early gods, through the heroes of epic, to the upper-class idols of Plutarch, and on to King Arthur and his Knights, to say nothing of the saints and martyrs of religion on the one hand, or the heroes of liberty and revolution on

[1] See Isaac Kramnick, *Bolingbroke and His Circle: The Politics of Nostalgia in the Age of Walpole* (Harvard, 1968); Hofstadter, *The Progressive Historians*, 23, 28, for comments by Parkman, Fiske, McMaster and Schouler, all conservative historians, on the horror of the times in which they lived. See also Edward Saveth, *American Historians and European Immigrants* (New York, 1948). Another refugee in a never-never land of the past is F. R. Leavis, whose picture of nineteenth-century England is as totally unrealistic as it must be emotionally satisfying.

the other.[1] The lives of men have been used at times in the subtlest, at others in the most obvious of ways to confirm attitudes and morality needed in the present. They have been used for noble purposes and for most disreputable ones. St William of Norwich, the boy saint, an innocent martyred by the Jews, was used for generation after generation to keep alive a bitter anti-Semitism. Not that this was mere hatred; it helped to explain, and therefore assuage, social frustration and personal disaster, to lift the burden of personal failure, to hang it like a millstone about the neck of the scapegoat. And yet, in contrast, we have Sir Galahad, a Chevalier Bayard, the glittering knight, *sans peur et sans reproche*; or the tougher, more profound, more desperate symbolism of Job. For the literate man of the Western world the past has been people to whom he has been tied by education as well as by tradition; active ghosts who lived permanently in his house of intellect and from whose influence it was hard to escape. Indeed, they were an integral and powerful part of that vast literary tradition which maintained its influence for centuries over the Western world. Victorian gentlemen, American as well as English, boomed the *Idylls of the King* to their listening families; Galahad, Lancelot, Guinevere and

[1] After her successful revolution, America needed a new past of her own and it is interesting to note that biography of heroes developed first, followed shortly afterwards by multi-volume annalistic history, from which historians began to move in the early twentieth century. See Hofstadter, *The Progressive Historians*, particularly chap. 1.

Arthur himself haunted them, as they had done their ancestors in the days of Malory. Indeed, the most remarkable aspect of Western ideology is its leech-like addiction to its past, expressed in personal terms. Men of the nineteenth century could speak of Job or Odysseus, of Catiline or Cicero, as if they had lived but yesterday. And, of course, they spoke of them as living entities, as symbols of situations, of actions that they themselves were involved in, or as examples of their own virtues or vices. These cult objects belonged to a living past. Their historicity was of little importance. Only a few professionals were concerned with their historical context, or wished to understand their lives by reference to their particular times and places, and see them as the result of precise social and political conditions which had vanished. They were the Pantheon of the ruling oligarchies of the West; like the gods in Sumer or Akkad, their fortunes varied. Who could have expected a revival of King Arthur and his knights amongst the solid middle-class merchants of Victorian Kensington, or that England's widowed Queen would have listened with rapt attention to the mournful voice of her Laureate as he recounted the deeds of Sir Lancelot and Queen Guinevere. And how odd it seems for Cicero to emerge suddenly in fifteenth-century Florence as the archetype of the dedicated citizen. However, his emergence proved to be in no way idiosyncratic. He remained a model of civic and political virtue for generations of oligarchs.[1] Of course, it was a Pantheon to which new gods were frequently elevated. Sir Francis Drake becomes a hero of Protestantism and manliness, his piracy, bankruptcy and bigotry decently forgotten; George Washington, his humanity nearly obliterated, is venerated as a model of moral rectitude, a man of adamantine honesty which, as with Drake – and this is important – *was rewarded.* Hence an excellent moral example. Naturally, as with the gods of old, the Pantheon possessed its wicked occupants, evil examples, its Neros, its Julians, its Borgias. And naturally nations made their own selections of good and bad; few were common, except the heroes of antiquity. With the perturbations of time and the shifting power within the ruling classes, the importance and significance of these examplars of the past have been changed or modified – a Cromwell or a Napoleon slip in and out of favour with the changing needs of the societies which gave them birth.[2] Nor is it surprising that, when the dispossessed began to achieve a sense of class and a capacity to articulate its hopes and despairs, they, too,

[1] For Cicero, see Hans Baron, *The Crisis of the Early Italian Renaissance* (2 vols., Princeton, 1955). Cicero's works were the only collection of a Latin author that the young Robert Walpole took with him to Eton; they were given to him by his father. They still remain in Sir Robert's library at Houghton, and quite obviously, from the scoring, he read them frequently.

[2] For changing attitudes to Napoleon, see P. Geyl, *Napoleon: For and Against* (1949). A similar study of Cromwell was badly needed and is now being undertaken: see *Past and Present*, no. 40 (1968),

should develop their own past and their own Pantheon – Robin Hood, John Ball, Ned Lud, to give the well-known British examples. But now in the Western world few are elected to the Pantheon; one or two, a Roosevelt, a Churchill, a Kennedy, reach the colonnade for a year or two, but the modern world is too critical, its knowledge too vast, its communications too rapid for them to enter the portals and be marmorealized. Of course this attitude to the past, of using historical figures as moral or social examples, still exists, particularly at the elementary stage of historical education, or amidst the more trivial historical literature of entertainment. But the declension is obvious if we think first of Malory's *Morte d'Arthur*, then of Tennyson's *Idylls of the King* and so to *Camelot*. From a myth charged with social emotion, it has become a night's musical entertainment. This use of the past has also been undermined, battered and exploded by the growth of history itself. I wish, however, to leave to a later chapter the effect of history on the vitality of the past as a social force. At present I am surveying the uses the past has been put to, and indicating whether or not such uses have a present efficacy. And obviously, the historical examplar is going the way of the historical annal.

187–91. Naturally Cromwell, along with Pym, Hampden and Sidney, was a favourite of the lower middle class with radical leanings who formed, in the nineteenth century, the audiences of Literary Institutions and Mechanics' Institutes.

Morality, political behaviour, civic virtue are now conceived in general, not personal or historic, terms. Even history textbooks, always the most conservative form of literature, are being recast; economic facts, social ideas, impersonal forces – these are dominating education, not the individual hero.[1] Here and there he survives, but rarely uncritically. The timeless heroes of the past are returning to their moments in time; diminished in stature, they are reabsorbed by the historic forces which moulded them.

But the past possessed, throughout the recorded history that we know, deeper purposes than moral or social example. Its influence on education was formidable, not only in the literate education of the priestly and noble classes, but also at the far lower levels of craftsmanship. Naturally, any society concerned with its social and religious stability will drill the young, not only in the tenets of the past, but also in its literature. The Chinese civil servants spent even longer than putative Roman Catholic priests in the study of their seminal texts and literature. In Augustan Rome, the world of Greece secured a like tyranny; in medieval Europe, either Eastern or Western, the fathers of the Church preoccupied the academic young for year after year. The Renaissance certainly broadened education, but did not change the direction to which it looked for its material or principles.

[1] J. H. Plumb, *Men and Places* (1963), 217–23, for a discussion of the present role of biography in historical studies.

Classical studies, language, grammar, philosophy, rhetoric, as well as literature and history, became the prime, if not sole, diet of generation after generation of schoolboys; the same curricula, the same insistence on antiquity, travelled to the New World and grew deep roots at Harvard and Yale.[1] And mathematics too, freer certainly from the strait-jacket of the past, were, in their elementary forms, dominated by the axioms and theorems of the ancients. As the needs of modern Europe became more complex, it is true that, alongside the dominant education system based on the past, there grew up a sub-system of modern languages, navigation, book-keeping – even, from the seventeenth century onwards, of elementary natural science, which catered for the needs of an expanding commercial society. But such teaching always bore the cachet of trade, not government, and so tended to be fostered, as in England, by socially dissident classes. Before the late nineteenth century it did not belong to the mainstream of education in the West.

The hold of the past on education has proved to be exceptionally formidable. Classical studies, if anything, strengthened in the nineteenth century, even in England where the Industrial Revolution, growing in power, was creating a new middle class for whom

[1] R. R. Bolgar, *The Classical Heritage and its Beneficiaries* (Cambridge, 1954).

the ancient system was peculiarly inappropriate.[1] However, manufacturers' sons from Manchester or Leeds struggled through their Homer and Virgil, plodded through the arid works of Livy or Xenophon and learned to translate Edmund Burke into a pastiche of Cicero. Younger sons of army officers and clergymen were dispatched to India with a thorough grounding in Plato and Aristotle and the Latin classics, to rule millions of peasants, knowing next to nothing of mathematics, economics, anthropology or sociology. Each had to learn the techniques necessary for his life's work *after* his major education was completed. That education was classical, backward-looking in the methods, materials and principles that it inculcated. Only in the twentieth century, when the full impact of the scientific revolution had hit Western society, has the past loosened its grip on the education of the young. It was only in the 1960s that scientists were released from the necessity of passing an examination in elementary Latin at my university – a reform which was violently and bitterly opposed. But computers and laboratories cannot wait. Even Euclid is going and so, too, the traditional problems of antique Islamic algebra. The new mathematics in the primary schools, the disappearance of

[1] Here the role of Thomas Arnold of Rugby was of great importance. See T. W. Bamford, *Thomas Arnold* (1960), 117-27. Although Arnold was not unaware of the economic importance of science, he believed that only the cultures of Greece and Rome were a proper study for gentlemen.

Latin and Greek from their central position, the encouragement of new disciplines, has destroyed the tyranny of the past. Education at long last is becoming squarely based on the needs and practices of the modern scientific world in which the West now has to dwell. But it is a movement from education for society, for government, for authority, to education in techniques. This is not all gain, for there has been a loss of a unifying ideology of social attitude which was implicit in an educational world dominated by the past. There is an immense difference between a discussion of Old Cato as the embodiment of civic virtue and one on the sociology of consent. One haunts the imagination, the other quickly fades. And in this period of vast and rapid transition there is great danger of a failure to secure an ideology of social attitude that can be taught and acceptably transmitted from generation to generation. As the past dies, and its hand grows palsied in its grip on religion, morality, education, there is a danger of social incoherence, of an idealization of analytic understanding rather than creative belief. And this loosening of the past in respect to education has subtler and more dangerous social consequences than those brought about by changes in the curriculum.

For centuries not only did learning depend on the past, but so did the crafts and skills of men. There were deeply traditional ways of doing things, from growing wheat to building a house, weaving cloth or smelting iron. And one learned these things from a master or one's father, who taught the methods which he had been taught. Technical change, of course, occurred, but it was slow in acceptance and perhaps even slower in diffusion, and it did not in any way affect the social structure of craft teaching or of the authority of tradition. The young worker lived in the household and learned his skills from its head; this transmission of traditional knowledge, of standards of workmanship as well as techniques, took place in the family, whether one was a son or an apprentice. Naturally this was weakened but not destroyed by the development of industry. Fathers took their sons down the mines or into the steelworks or on to the shipyards. Even in textiles the young hands were taught by old hands, and because many mechanical methods lasted for more than a generation, the skill taught by one's father or master endured for a lifetime. This the scientific revolution has drastically changed. The skills by which men and women earn their bread can no longer be learned at home. They cannot be handed down from generation to generation. Nowadays they are taught that they may, throughout their lives, have to discard much of their learning and re-learn their craft time and time again. Think but of radio sets or of motor-cars and how they have changed in less than a generation. So men and women today are not conditioned in their daily lives to a world that is tied to an imperceptibly changing past, in which the patterns of work, the relationship between fathers and children, or even between the social classes, possess the sanctity of tradition. Life is change, uncertainty, and only the present can have validity and that, maybe, not for long. The consequence, of course, is to accept a similar attitude in ideas of conduct, in the concepts of social structure or family life. They can be judged by what they do, but lack validity because they have been. So we are witnessing the dissolution of the conditions which tied man to his past and gave him his Janus face.

Once the vice-like grip of the past is loosened in religion, in education, in economic activity, then a paralysis in social matters quickly sets in. It is not too wanton to see one result of the decay of personal direct education between man and apprentice, or father and son, or mother and daughter for that matter, in the decay of the family structure and the growing independence of adolescent life. To so many young men and women the ideology of the family is often no more than a hollow collection of outworn concepts to which adults themselves pay scant attention. Similarly, the attitudes between the sexes have been conditioned by the antique past. Augustan Rome, in this respect, was not remarkably different from Victorian Boston. The woman was subordinate, primarily a wife and mother, confined within the limits of domesticity. And sexually she was totally subordinate – overt wantonness deprived her of respect. And even if aristocratic élites did, from time to time, depart from these attitudes, it was rarely for long, and the bulk of the ruling classes never did so. The sanctions of the past lay heavily on marriage; they are rapidly crumbling. The same is true of other sexual activity. It is no longer controlled by inherited historical morality, or, where it is, the control is weak; biological urges, compulsive needs, statistically proved, guide us to toleration and, perhaps, back to our humanity. The taboos of the dead no longer cast their shadows across the bed. To me this loosening of time's stranglehold is far from wholly bad. The past in its personal as well as its social dimension has been full of nightmares.

Wherever we look, in all areas of social and personal life, the hold of the past is weakening. Rituals, myths, the need for personal roots in time are so much less strong than they were a mere hundred or even fifty years ago. In education and economic activity the past has ceased to be a guide to the present, even if bits of it still litter and hamper the development of both. In family and sexual relations the past offers little understanding and no comfort. Of course there are areas of resistance, but they are islands of conviction in a surging sea of doubt. In these aspects, at least, if the past is not dead, the rattle of death can be heard.

Over the centuries, however, men always turned

to the past for more than a guide to the authority of the present. They thought that by its study they could discern the future, and maybe even predict it. They discovered repetitions, unfolding purpose, inevitable consequences in their study of it. The weakening of the past's hold on society does not necessarily mean that this function, or use of the past, has also ceased to have value or has lost its relevance. How far is it still tenable to consider that the past holds the key to the future? Or that by its study man can control it? We must consider the past as destiny.

2

THE PAST
AS DESTINY

THE past in relation to human destiny is a vast and
complex subject. Religion by its very nature is in-
extricably involved with the past regarded as destiny. In all early societies for which we have records,
there were immortal gods whose relations with men
in the past naturally threw light on their attitudes in
the present. With self-confidence that no experience
could daunt, priests interpreted the earlier behaviour
of the gods in order to predict the fate of individual
men in the future. Heaven, hell, rebirth or oblivion,
each religion possessed a built-in pattern of destiny,
some complex, some simple, some capable of change
and variety, others immutable for century after century. Yet for many of these religions the past was a
huge catalogue of examples which were rarely involved in the historical process as such. I shall say
very little about these religions, except for Christianity, which required a much more historical commit-
ment than any other religion.

However, to return to the question of destiny,
very early in man's story he tried to predict the future

precisely; to study events, portents, omens in their repetition and in their subtle distinctions in order to get a line on the future, or to interpret the intentions of the gods who, he knew well enough, could be both hostile and fickle. The earliest written records of Ancient China are the oracle bones of An-yang – a huge library of divination by which the Chinese sages, by studying the cracks in burnt tortoise-shells, could read the nature of future events, or at least decide whether times might be auspicious or not for a particular activity.[1] And naturally, without a vast library of reference, such divination lacked validity. Each prognostication had to be made in the light of earlier forecasts and then, when made, filed away for future reference. In Ancient Mesopotamia no step of any importance was taken by kings, governors or priests without consulting the omens, interpretations of which were recorded and filed for hundreds and hundreds of years. They were available for use to diviners for more than a thousand years after the event for which they had been used. By such an intensive study of the conjunction of an omen with an event, the Assyrians thought that the future might be controlled by the past. And from the oracle bones of An-yang

---

[1] The official historian in China seems to have evolved, during the Han period, from the office of the Grand Astrologer, by which title Ssu-ma Chi'en's father was known. For a description of the way tortoise-shells were used, see *The Complete Works of Chuang Tzu*, transl. Burton Watson (Columbia University Press, 1968), 298.

and the omen tablets of Old Babylon to the dialectical materialism of Marx, Engels and Lenin, the same optimistic hope that the study of the past will enable one to control the future everywhere abounds.

Naturally, in societies that were predominantly agrarian, the stars were soon put to their uses. Men rapidly observed that the waxing and waning of constellations indicated a change in the seasons, that the stars foretold when the Nile might flood or the rains come, as in China or in the Yucatan. So perfect a correspondence of events pointed to an obvious, and to the primitive mind an eminently rational, theory, that the stars in their conjunction influenced the lives of men. Few human beliefs, even when they have been demonstrated to be ludicrous and absurd, have possessed stronger roots or a more persistent life. And, of course, the study of the stars in relation to the past and the future produced far more than astrology. It led men whose intelligence, whose capacity for original and scientific thought was every bit as good as that of our most gifted men, to devise clocks, astrolabes and orrerys of the most scientific and delicate complexity.[1] The dominance of the past does not

---

[1] J. Needham, Wang Ling and D. J. de Solla Price, *Heavenly Clockwork* (Cambridge, 1960); also J. Needham, *Time and the Eastern Man*, Royal Anthropological Institute of Great Britain and Ireland, Occasional Papers, no. 21 (London, 1965), 17–19; J. Needham, *Science and Civilization in China* (Cambridge, 1965), iv (2) 465–80. The most elaborate and complex astronomic clock of the T'ang dynasty appears to have been devised so that the position of the stars

mean a static world without technical change or social transformation. Indeed, no civilization has looked so resolutely backwards as the Chinese, yet the technical ingenuity of the Chinese was quite remarkable and often well in advance of Western

---

would be known even if the Heavens were cloudy, in case any of the Emperor's wives or concubines conceived. Also, D. J. de Solla Price, *Science since Babylon* (New Haven, 1961). Criticism of some of Needham's claims will be found in Carlo M. Cipolla, *Clocks and Culture, 1300-1700* (1967), 152, but he does not deny the elaboration of the Chinese astronomical instruments. The whole problem of the social environment needed to promote scientific investigation and technical discovery is still a vital and unsolved problem for the historian of society as well as of science. See J. Needham, 'Science and Society in East and West', *Science and Society* (New York, 1964), xxviii 385-408; 'Poverties and Triumphs of the Chinese Scientific Tradition', in *Scientific Change*, ed. A. C. Crombie (London, 1963), 117-49. The explosive nature of this subject was further demonstrated by the controversy which followed the publication of J. E. C. Hill, *The Intellectual Origins of the English Revolution* (Oxford, 1965), for the most important critical reviews of which see H. R. Trevor-Roper, *History and Theory* (Middletown, 1966), v 61-82, and A. R. Hall, 'The Scientific and Puritan Revolution', *History* (1965), 332-7.

A similar outburst followed the publication of B. Herzen's article 'On the Social and Economic Roots of Newton's *Principia*', in *Science at the Crossroads* (1932). Although many of the criticisms offered to these pieces of Marxist analysis by Hill and Herzen are valid enough, the fact remains that the transition from a backward-looking society, with an ideology weighted down by tradition, concepts and examples of the past, to a forward-looking, scientifically orientated society is likely to be the result of socio-economic circumstances as well as intellectual developments; otherwise the history of Babylon, Greece and China must have been quite different, unless one is willing to accept the operation of pure chance or the finger of Divine Providence. There is not room here to deal adequately with this problem, although the subject under discussion is germane to it.

societies whose relationship with their pasts was less systematized and less all-embracing. However, astronomy, unlike astrology, was a matter only for priests and sages so that they could render their ritual more precise or forecast the heavenly movements more accurately. The majority of men and women, both educated and illiterate, were concerned only with astrological aspects of the stars, what indeed they might foretell. And here the past was as potent as it was relevant. For conjunctions were linked with events, propitious or disastrous as the case might be. Each individual's horoscope was not an exercise of imagination, but the result of complex historical observation.[1] And once the basic premise was accepted that the position of the planets and the stars directly influenced the nature of men and their actions, their luck or lack of it, astrology acquired a firm rationality. Century after century, men of the highest intelligence could accept this living influence of the past, an influence indeed which did not only live, but foretold the future – indeed controlled it. Even at the height of the scientific revolution, in the days of the foundation of the Royal Society in London, at the time when Newton was writing his *Principia*, the Earl of

---

[1] See Helmut Rehder, '*Planetenkinder*', *The Graduate Journal* (University of Texas, Austin 1968), viii 69-97, for a discussion of the complex involvement of astrological concepts in art and literature by the sixteenth century. The subject is vast, and later centuries, i.e. the seventeenth, eighteenth and nineteenth, are largely neglected by social historians.

Shaftesbury, the close friend of John Locke who lived in his household, believed implicity in astrology and was convinced that his entire life had been foretold, because it was fore-ordained, by a Dutch astrologer.[1] Nor did belief die in the age of Enlightenment. Certainly it became entangled in the esoteric doctrines of Swedenborgians, Illuminati, Masons and the like in which so many educated and sophisticated men of this century dabbled.[2] By then this star-haunted past had lost some of its social force, and had become a past of semi-credulity, that world of half-belief in which leisured dilettanti took so much delight. By the nineteenth century it was largely driven out of educated society, but it remained important, along with oracles and magic stories, with the poorly educated or illiterate classes. And in twentieth-century London the majority of daily papers still publish their astrologists' divinations, the attitude of the mass now being largely that of the eighteenth-century aristocracy – a mild fascination laced with disbelief.

The role of the past in divination and astrology was

[1] Bishop Burnet, *History of His Own Time* (2nd ed., Oxford, 1833), i 175. Shaftesbury was in no way singular for his age.

[2] See F. R. Dumas, *Cagliostro* (Paris, 1966), and Casanova's *Memoirs*. It should be noted, however, that all of these cults rested heavily on antiquity, on Egyptian magic and the like. After all, the Masons required Solomon's Temple and bogus antique rituals to bolster their beliefs. See also Erik Iversen, *The Myth of Egypt and its Hieroglyphs* (Copenhagen, 1961).

largely compilatory, the provision of arcane knowledge which might enable a Taoist magician, a
Babylonian divinator or a Delphic priestess to achieve
a successful prophecy. The study of the stars did not
involve a deeper process at work in the past itself, or
discern in the nature of man and his society a dynam-
ism that was impelling him towards the future; it only
laid bare a mechanism of exceptional intricacy and
obscurity that needed only to be closely and contin-
uously observed in order to be understood. It was a
code to be deciphered, not a process to be understood.[1] The concept that within the history of mankind itself a process was at work which would mould
his future, and lead man to situations totally different
from his past, seems to have found its first expression
amongst the Jews. The Greeks had a healthy sense of
their own superiority – more, perhaps, than most
ancient people – yet they possessed no belief that their
history taught them they had a special destiny and a
special future, or that, whatever might be their tri-
bulations and defects, the wondrous portents of their
past showed the special interest of God in their
destiny. The Jews, however, came to believe very
early in their history that not only themselves but also
their own special God had superiority over all others;

---

[1] The idea that the past contains a code to be unlocked is a very
constantly recurring theme in the history of ideas; the Book of Revelation often and the Egyptian Pyramids occasionally have been
thought to contain the key.

so long as his people kept his commands, his very special commands to them as Israelites, then their destiny would be glorious, the Messiah would come. And the proof of this special destiny lay in the events and in the prophecies which their records contained, records which took them back through Moses to Abraham and the patriarchs and so to the first man and the first woman created by God. Both their history and their genealogy were specially sanctified. Other races might be ruled by god-like kings or by princes and priests who could trace their lines back to the gods, but for the Jews the position was even more special, more select. Their line went back to the one true God who had demonstrated over and over again, in event after event, that all other gods were false. So, with the Jews, the past became more than a collection of tales, a projection of human experience, or a system of moral examples; far more, indeed, than a collection of annals, genealogies or rites, although it combined all of these things. It became an intimate part of destiny, and an interpretation of the future, more certain, more absolute, more comprehensive than any divination either by the stars or oracles could ever be.

Ultimately the idea of a historical continuum from the creation prevailed. All other interests including the interest in non- Hebrew history were sacrificed to it. A privileged line of events represented and signified the continuous intervention of God in the world he had created.[1]

And because of its totality, because it combined the whole of life, past, present and future, its capacity to dominate the minds of men was immensely strengthened. The uniqueness of this concept lay in the idea of development. The past was no longer static, a mere store of information, example and event, but dynamic, an unfolding story.

But this social need for the past, for its events and its prophecies, did not lead to any great historical skill on the part of the Jews.[2] They needed the past – certain events, certain circumstances, certain prophecies which would enable them to believe in the ultimate purpose of God and the destiny of Israel. They were not concerned, however, to analyse history except for its prophetic qualities, nor indeed to record anything but that which illustrated the will of Yahweh or the insight of his prophets.[3]

The distinctive beliefs of the Jews did not, however, affect the attitude of the ancient world towards the past for many centuries. It caused the Jews difficulties, certainly, culminating in the violent struggle against

[1] A. Momigliano, 'Time in Ancient Historiography', *History and Theory* (Middletown, 1966), Beiheft 6, 18–19.

[2] Ibid. 19. As Momigliano points out, the Jews were ordered to remember the past (Deut. vii 18), and they did, e.g. Psalm cv.

[3] Hence the extremely difficult historical problems created by much of the prophetic writing of the Old Testament or of the Dead Sea Scrolls.

the Romans, the destruction of their Temple and their dispersal.[1] Their own highly individual use of the past became ideologically revolutionary only when, transmogrified by Christianity, it became part of the belief of an established Church, backed by the authority of the state – a revolution of exceptional importance, one of the most profound that Western man has experienced in the field of ideas.

Christianity welded the past and the future together, not merely for a tribe or a people, but for the whole of mankind. Like Judaism, it was exclusive. All other gods were false, all other beliefs wicked. But unlike Judaism, its emphasis rested firmly on belief rather than law. The brotherhood of men was implicit in all that it taught. Its God might be exclusive, but its message was not. And it was far more personal, far more closely orientated towards the individual. It made the past an intimate part of each person's destiny – not merely the nation's. It was, however, both the Jews and the Christians who gave a new significance to life. Their beliefs stressed the sense of event leading to event, and from this grew the idea of an unfolding destiny, that the whole purpose of life could be read from the past, by what had happened.

Although the Jews had long held this view, it was not immediately adopted by the first Christians, for whom the past was irrelevant. The Messiah had

[1] Josephus, *The Jewish War*, ed. M. I. Finley (New York, 1965), xvi–xviii.

71

arrived, been crucified, resurrected; his life and death announced the imminent coming of the Kingdom of God. Time would shortly end, and human history close. For such believers the past was without significance. Furthermore, the early Christians do not seem to have used the historical facts of Jesus's life as an argument against the pagans, to prove the authenticity of their religion.[1] St. Paul and his converts based their belief and their attitudes on the transcendental nature of Christ, who was ever living and therefore independent of any historical context. However, this theological interpretation was narrowed by the Gospel writers, for a variety of reasons, to an historical account, giving rise to the most fundamental historical concept in Christianity – the time before Christ and the time after. And, of course, the time after presented the greatest difficulties. Time passed and Christ obstinately failed to reappear, the Kingdom of Heaven remained in the wings of Time and the Kingdom of Men dominated the stage. The Day of Doom had to be projected further and further into the future, even though it was never distant by our standards of time. Until the nineteenth century the past was

[1] S. G. F. Brandon, *History, Time and Deity* (Manchester, 1965), 160 ff., and especially 160 n. 2. For the development of ideas about history in early Christianity, see also Erich Dinkler, 'Earliest Christianity', in *The Idea of History in the Ancient Near East*, ed. Robert C. Dentan (New Haven, 1955), 171–214. Also C. H. Dodd, *History and the Gospel* (1938); Oscar Cullmann, *Christ and Time*, trans. F. V. Filson (rev. ed., 1962).

very short; so in the earlier centuries was the future. This being so, the Christians were forced to develop an elaborate theology and an even more elaborate eschatology. This required the past to justify an institution which could control and help fulfil the Christian mission, namely, an organized Church with a hierarchy of bishops, priests and deacons capable of interpreting the present condition of men in the light of the Christian past.

By the conversion of Constantine, the Western world was Christianized, and neither pagan counter-attack nor barbarian invasion interrupted for long the forward march of the Church. And, furthermore, the intellectual élite of the Christian Church, its scholars, theologians, philosophers, propagandists, was to achieve and maintain a settled orthodoxy of thought with the force and authority of secular government behind them. This transformation from a pagan to a Christian ideology created formidable problems, more formidable even than those which were to face the Protestant apologists at the time of the Reformation. Not only was there the problem of the destruction of popular culture – the uprooting of temples, local gods, the cults and rituals that went with them – a task which proved, in the end, almost hopeless, for although the superstructure of popular paganism could be brought crashing to the ground by state laws and savage actions, it was beyond the powers of either Church or state to eradicate totally the magical beliefs of the multitude. They lingered on in the limbo of folklore, or were absorbed into Christianity. Indeed, the early Fathers semi-deliberately brought about the transmogrification of many pagan spirits. They could do no other. The phantom world of Christianity was soon populated with flocks of saints and hordes of demons.[1] Nevertheless, the formal practices and cults of magic or of oracular interpretation were destroyed and, in theory at least, the Fathers were adamant in their detestation of all forms of magic, black or white.[2] And as far as the state was concerned, the elaborate divinatory systems of Babylon or of Delphi or of Rome were reduced to the whispered tales of old wives and hucksters. The upper-class ideology of the ancient world, its methods of interpreting life and history, were torn down. Some seepage there may have been from the Stoics, from Plato via the Neo-Platonists, and elsewhere, but the revolution in ideas was more dramatic, more far-reaching, more absolute than that experienced by any other great civilization. New religions came to India, to China or to Japan, but they were

---

[1] See A. A. Barb, 'The Survival of Magic Arts', in *The Conflict between Paganism and Christianity in the Fourth Century,* ed. A. Momigliano (Oxford, 1963), 100–25. The Council of Laodicea forbade the exaggerated cult of angels. The miraculous survived. In the sixth century a cloud of Irish saints walked across the Bristol Channel and roosted in the villages of north Devon and Cornwall. Like wonders occurred throughout Christendom.

[2] Ibid., 107.

absorbed. Only Islam had the same quality of ideological revolution as Christianity, but this took place
amongst primitive and tribal peoples.

The intellectual problems of the Early Fathers
were far greater, of course, than the mere destruction
of divination and magic. The central theme of
history was now Christian and Jewish, leading back
through Christ to David, Moses, Abraham to Adam,
which presented a severe problem for other histories
and other chronologies.[1] The manufacture of a past
which gave a predominant and decisive role to
Jewish history, with which Roman and Greek events
and personalities were linked, was but one half of a
difficult problem. The unfolding narrative did not
end with Christ. The Second Coming was delayed
and delayed and delayed, so the past had to be used to
project the future in more complex ways. It had to
be lived within terms of the Christian past. There is
no need to discuss the way that the Day of Judgment

[1] Orosius (c. 417) provided the final amalgam of pagan and Christian history in a form regarded as entirely suitable for the Christian
world, but it was the end of a long process begun in Alexandria in
the second century. Naturally it became easier to accomplish as
paganism died, its books obliterated or forgotten. But it was only
achieved by ignoring a great deal of the history of the ancient world.
'No real Christian historiography founded on the political experience
of Herodotus, Thucydides, Livy and Tacitus was transmitted to the
Middle Ages': A. Momigliano, 'Pagan and Christian Historiography
in the Fourth Century A.D.', in *The Conflict between Paganism and
Christianity in the Fourth Century*, 89. The crucial figure in the
development of a Christian chronology was Eusebius, for whom
see D. S. Wallace-Hadrill, *Eusebius of Caesarea* (1960), 155–67.

was pushed further and further into the future, nor to investigate the explanations which the Fathers gave for this process, but they required, in order to do it, the active use of the past. Now that Christianity had triumphed, the future could only be explained in historical terms. The fact of the delay of Christ's coming, and the relative youthfulness of their religion compared with the cults of antiquity, were dangerous breeding-grounds for scepticism. Two arguments were needed and both were used. The Old Testament became as essential as the New to Christianity for it revealed the purpose of Christ's God stretching back long before His birth, which gave Christianity an antiquity and a sanction that antedated the pagan world in its entirety. You could not get further back than Adam. This was Tertullian's view. The other argument used to still doubt was that since Christ the Church had been fulfilling its mission, indeed His mission. It had spread, grown, converted, succeeded. Time was essential for God's purpose of conversion. Yet to prove this needed history, ecclesiastical history such as Eusebius provided, to underscore to the doubtful what was obvious to the converted. The catastrophes that overtook the secular world – the almost total collapse of the West – created a further problem which St Augustine tackled with enduring success. No matter how cataclysmic the ruin of the state might be, this was only to be expected, considering man's sinful nature. However, this was but transitory, the result of and punishment for sin; ultimately the City of God, the community of the faithful, would triumph as God's purpose was revealed at the predestined end of Time. And this community grew even as the world decayed. History proved it.

From this time onwards Western and Eastern Europe were dominated by a past that was in marked contrast to the past which had dominated earlier civilizations, the Greek or Roman worlds, or even the contemporary civilizations of China or India. It was, if one may use the term, a narrative past, a past with sharp and positive beginnings – indeed, it started at a precise moment in time – a story of unfolding events, revealing the purpose of God and man leading up to the dramatic climax of Christ's life and death; after this the pilgrimage of mankind to its final Doom, which would also come at a precise moment in time. And this narrative aspect of man's destiny was made visible; it was depicted on the walls of churches, enshrined in rituals, enacted in miracle plays. This sense of narrative and of unfolding purpose bit deeply into European consciousness. It brought easy acceptance of the idea not only of change but also of development. More importantly still, it implied the necessity of progress – spiritual progress, certainly not secular for many centuries, but the seed was there, even though dormant. It only required favourable circumstances to quicken it with life. The past acquired a dynamic, almost a propulsion, which it did not acquire elsewhere. It became easy enough for a Christian to regard his own life in the same dramatic terms, as an unfolding, as possessing a purpose, a mission, a destined end. That is the purpose of God, and the purpose of individual life became identical – again unique and revolutionary.

After St Augustine, the first great seminal period in which man had remoulded his concepts of the past was over. And, in consequence, there was a rapid diminution in the output of historical explanation and propaganda. This was aided by the barbarization of the West, which led to a more primitive ideological world, and to something of a resurrection of pagan beliefs in Christian guise, an aspect of the past which had seized the imagination of many of the Fathers. This past of saints and devils and miracle-working relics flourished apace. Hagiography, the tales of saints and wonders, became the most widespread literature dealing with the past. But the sense of mission, of historic destiny, was always there. And although historians have sought for the origins of aggressive individualism in the Protestant ethic, it is to my mind embedded in the basic historical concepts which emerged in the first centuries of Christian activity.

The medieval West, however, inherited from the Early Fathers the concept that the Church was an institution whose power and authority were historically based and therefore historically justifiable. Documentary record acquired sanctity; the acts of councils, bishops, popes needed not only preservation but commentary. In conflicts with heretical or schismatic institutions, in its struggle with secular authority, the Church based its arguments over and over again on its historical records. As with the divinators of Babylon, or the sages and astrologers of China, the past acquired for canonists and jurists an absolute sanction. Indeed, at times they needed it so badly that they forged it.[1] Pope Stephen II, for example, had no hesitation in sending Pepin, King of the Franks, a letter in St Peter's own handwriting which confirmed Papal possession of Lombard territories conquered by Pepin. The preservation of records acquired economic and constitutional significance for popes, emperors, abbots, barons, priests. They became the weapons of authority.

[1] For the activity of forgers in the Middle Ages and the credulity with which the ancient charters were accepted, see H. Fuhrmann, 'Die Falschungen im Mittelalten', *Historische Zeitschrift* (1963), cxcvii 529-54. Naturally this was challenged, but see Fuhrmann's vigorous riposte, ibid. 580-601. See also W. Ullmann, *A History of Political Thought: The Middle Ages* (1965), 80-85: 'The aim of these forgers – and considering the extent of their fabrications there must have been whole ateliers of workers – was to buttress the hierocratic thesis by surrounding it with the halo of antiquity. As with most medieval forgeries, they did not in many cases invent anything out of the blue, but clothed an already virtually accepted thesis in the garb of an ancient decree.' Three-quarters of the imperial decrees of the Benedictus Levita are false: ibid. 83-84. Even when exposed, forgeries continued

The true material of history began to be accumulated long, long before there were historians of sufficient sophistication to use it, in marked contrast to the ancient world where Herodotus, Thucydides, Livy were embarrassed by its absence. The past in the West had acquired more than respect, it had acquired sanctity. The ideology, however, remained always more important than the material which justified it. And the past possessed deep religious significance, not only for emperors and kings, popes and bishops, but also for the whole of humanity. Each man was involved in a universal historical drama. The forces of Satan were at large, embattled maybe, constantly attacked and occasionally overwhelmed by the forces of God, yet Satan in this wicked world, particularly suited for his evil, had his triumphs. The war still had to be fought. And this great battle against evil, which

---

to be accepted; the past was too valuable to be rejected on merely sceptical grounds, hence the exposure of the Donation of Constantine (c. 1000) by John the Deacon had no long-term results, although it influenced the actions of Otto III. The time was not propitious. It was, however, in the more sceptical age of Lorenzo Valla four hundred years later, when its exposure created a sensation, but then the past was being assailed and reconstructed. The belief in, and market for holy relics - the past made visible - led, as with charters, to their being forged and manufactured in quantity; there was enough True Cross to build a galleon, and at one time twelve foreskins of Christ were being venerated, one in the Pope's own church of St John Lateran. For the Donation of Constantine, see Ullmann, op. cit. 97-98; for relics, G. Rattray Taylor, *Sex in History* (1953), 42-43; also H. C. Lea, *Studies in Church History* (Philadelphia, 1883), 46-61.

could not, men hoped, last much longer, was clearly visible from any backward glance at man's history. From Adam's expulsion and Abel's murder it was as clear as daylight. The past revealed the nature of the Devil and his wiles; and the past of the Church, its time-proven morality, showed how he might be contained. So active a past seeped through the interstices of society, straining all thought, creating veneration for customs, traditions and inherited wisdom; and so a bulwark was set up against innovation and change unless it could be clothed in antique guise, as a recapture of a purer or holier past. Yet profound as the respect for the past was in all medieval thinkers and theologians, in men of action as well as in men of contemplation, it never became all-embracing or rendered learning or enquiry totally static. It never dominated the European world to the degree that it did the Chinese. The European past remained dynamic, a past of struggle, change, defeat, victory – a past which moved with and in Time, therefore usable in aggression, serviceable for conquest, for crusading zeal. The Church might base its authority on its antiquity, but it remained also a Church militant, with a purpose and a destiny, a future explicit from its past.

At the time of the Renaissance and Reformation, the vast historical justification of the Church, which had come to embrace almost the entire ideology of the Western world, was subject to criticism and attack. The attack, however, concentrated on specific issues such as the forged Donation of Constantine upon which so much of the authority of the Church depended, or the primacy of the Bishop of Rome, and not on the basic religious myth which gave the past its essential structure. The core of Christian belief remained; indeed it was fortified. True, the Italian humanists rediscovered Herodotus and Thucydides, Livy and Tacitus, and Machiavelli brooded on Livy's *Discorsi*. Both he and Guicciardini extracted themselves to a remarkable degree from the compact framework of Christian myth; yet their use of the past was similar in method, if not in intention, to earlier writers, particularly the Ancients to whom they felt very close.[1]

Nor was the Christian myth fractured or transformed by the Reformation. It merely underwent

[1] They did not wish to understand the past in its own terms. They wanted to use it for political ends, for it to serve statesmen as it had hitherto served moralists as a guide to conduct. Yet, in many ways, modern historical study stems from their work and the work of their contemporaries. Machiavelli's threat to the Christian past was not immediately recognized, but once the Counter-Reformation was under way his name began to arouse horror and detestation in orthodox circles. See Felix Raab, *The English Face of Machiavelli* (1964), 3-4. See also A. Momigliano, 'Pagan and Christian Historiography in the Fourth Century A.D.' in *The Conflict between Paganism and Christianity in the Fourth Century*, 89: 'When in the fifteenth and sixteenth centuries the humanists rediscovered their Herodotus, Thucydides, Livy and Tacitus, they rediscovered something for which there was no plain Christian alternative . . . The models for political and military history remained irretrievably pagan.'

modification – at least for the growing mass of the literate world. In a few scholarly circles, and in matters which involved historical debate of a precise order, the first glimmers of a new attitude were to be discerned – at first in France with Baudouin, La Popelinière and Bodin, Sarpi in Venice, and Selden, Camden and the antiquaries in England. But to these I must return later.

But as an example of how the past was used in strictly Christian and dogmatic terms in Protestant countries after the Reformation, there is no better case history than England. Also, this possesses the further interest that it exported its vision of the past to New England in the seventeenth century, where it was to have a formidably long life. As with the Fathers, or, indeed, many medieval writers, the propagandists of the English Reformation saw history as a conflict between God and the angels and the Devil and his demons, who, though doomed to lose, possessed ingenuity, gained temporary successes and all too frequently baffled and deluded a gullible and sinful humanity. Indeed, the Devil's most artful work had been to found the Catholic Church and impose on a credulous world the great Antichrist of Rome. The saints of the Church of Rome might be no more than rank superstition, but the Protestant martyrs were real enough. Their burning flesh, their broken limbs and torn entrails were recorded in majestic prose by John Foxe, whose *Actes and Monuments,* published in 1563, became a second Bible. It stressed what to Foxe and his followers was obvious – that in the great work of salvation, of reformation, of securing Christ's Kingdom, the English had a special role.[1] They were, indeed, the new Israel, as Oliver Cromwell a hundred years later was to tell them over and over again, whether they were butchering Catholics at Drogheda or Calvinists at Dunbar.[2]

It is not surprising that the Bible and Foxe's *Martyrs,* as the book came to be called, should be joined by a third, John Bunyan's *Pilgrim's Progress,* which allegorized in personal terms man's Christian destiny. Tribulation, pain, suffering, endless temptation were man's lot, and yet by fortitude and God's grace he might hope for salvation and success. The past, even a man's life, still possessed an unfolding drama which the future would complete. There was in all men, as in all history, manifest destiny. And these three books were often the only books which the illiterate, the semi-literate and the literate poor ever knew in any detail. And the richness of their imagery, the vividness of their narratives, burnt this sense of progress and destiny into the unconscious mind of the British people. It was, in essence, the Christian past of St Augustine and the Fathers; still

---

[1] William Haller, *Foxe's Book of Martyrs and the Elect Nation* (1963).

[2] A habit that he acquired from his Puritan preacher who appropriated the Old Testament and plundered it for examples of God's violence to the unrighteous.

that dramatic Christian purposeful past which had won its victories a thousand years earlier. The time came, however, when it needed a secular cousin. It spawned one with ease. The vast growth of the British Empire, the fabulous wealth that poured into England in the eighteenth and nineteenth centuries, the almost constant success in battle, underlined, if underlining were to be needed, that England had a special destiny created for it by Providence. And even if, amongst more sophisticated minds, Providence. was quietly dropped, the sense of manifest destiny was not. The Protestant martyrs were changed for English heroes – Drake and Raleigh and Hawkins, Clive in India and Wolfe at Quebec – and beyond, further back, even in the mists of time, the same early British heroes could be discerned – Alfred, and beyond him Caractacus. One has only to open the pages of J. R. Green's *History of the English People* to see how easily Foxe's attitude to the past could influence a national history.

There were, of course, subtler forms of the concept that the past indicated a special destiny for the race. There evolved in England during the seventeenth century, largely after 1660, when the crude and dramatic concept of England as a New Israel had begun to fade, a theory of the past that was to strengthen over the next two centuries. It has been called the Whig interpretation of history, but this is a misnomer. It completely pervaded the ideology of the British establishment, Whig or Tory, over the eighteenth, nineteenth and twentieth centuries. It formed Churchill's mind as well as Burke's; indeed, it sustained Churchill's deepest convictions. Already bruised and battered by academic scholarship, nevertheless it remained full of potency and played an effective part in Britain's concept of its own role in the titanic struggle against Hitler.[1] This was the belief that English institutions, like no other in the Western world, were the result of slow growth from Saxon days; that, like a coral reef, precedent had fallen on precedent, erecting a bulwark of liberty, creating institutions such as Parliament or constitutional monarchy. Many centuries and much tribulation had been required to bring these to perfection; their antiquity, their slow growth, endowed them with a special virtue, and British history, therefore, was a moral as well as a political example to mankind. Not only did these beliefs achieve an almost universal currency amongst politicians, clerics, civil servants, and navy officers, but they were most actively preached to the artisans and clerks who made up the lower middle class. Dean Farrar, the pupil of Thomas Arnold, the great headmaster of Rugby, and author of the excruciatingly sentimental *Eric, or Little by Little*, was an ardent proselytizer of the providential nature of England's history, and his rich rhetoric

[1] See my 'Churchill, Historian', in *Churchill: Four Faces and the Man* (1969), particularly, pp. 119-24, 149-51.

rolled round the Literary Institutions that proliferated in London's suburbs. He told his audience at Harrow's Literary Institution on 13 October 1857:

> Through the confusions of nations, the great idea of humanity lives and grows: from the soil of deciduous peoples and decaying races springs up the mightly bole of the great people of England, greater, better, more perfect than the peoples out of which it grew – The Briton bequeathed us his faith and awe; the Roman his laws and order; the Saxon his freedom and manliness; the Dane his strength and intrepidity; the Norman his cultivation and enterprise. They died, and passed away; and we, the children of all of them, are nobler than any. 'We are the heirs of all the ages in the foremost files of Time.'[1]

Each great civilization had been, according to Farrar, ordained by Providence to a particular task:

> Every nation has had some work to do: Greece, ere she perished, wrought into perfection the idea of beauty. Rome perfected the conception of order: Judea disseminated the knowledge of Inspiration. Other nations too have had their work, and doing it or failing in it have passed away.[2]

This national past could be used with the great Christian past. They were not in any way inimical to each other. God could be British, or French or

[1] Rev. F. W. Farrar, *The People of England* (n.d.), 36.
[2] Ibid. 7.

German or Spanish or American, as well as Christian. And like the Christian past this nationalist past could be adjusted to the vulgar. It could be couched in jingoistic forms to arouse the mob, and yet it was capable of very subtle expression, supported as it was by a remarkable academic apparatus of persuasive argument as well as a philosophic justification in the magnificent rhetoric of Burke. Mortally wounded, certainly dying, yet this myth still exists, and still exerts force; little perhaps in sophisticated historical circles, but in the middle-class reading public of England it still provides support for their bruised and damaged egos.

Nor should we think that England alone is prone to such uses of the past. They are a European common-place of the last three hundred years, a natural result of aggressive nationalism. Manifest destiny in many forms, crude or subtle, we can see at work in France and in Germany, in the last hundred years even in Italy. Mostly they are cruder than the English form and have been, except in Germany, accepted less uniformly in academic circles. And similar myths were at work in America. The strict Calvinist past – the past of the Bible, of Foxe, of the New Israel – reached its final, sad conclusion with Jonathan Edwards.[1] This death of a theological past did not free America from its sense of special providential destiny. The religious

[1] Peter Gay, *A Loss of Mastery: Puritan Historians in Colonial America* (California University Press, 1966).

past donned a secular overcoat.[1] This new secular past was fortified by the events of the American Revolution, which seemed a unique event, even after France's revolution had followed, for that had been stained by Terror and dictatorship. The historians of the nineteenth century, the great romantics – Bancroft, Motley, Prescott and Parkman – felt, like William Bradford, that America was cleaner, purer, less corrupt and more in the way of God and godliness than the evil world which had been left behind in Europe. Indeed, America was to be the tribunal before which all history was to be judged.[2] Although these historians were reasonably accurate in their narrative for the time at which they wrote, and hung original documents on their works like banners, yet they were not really historians. They were manufacturers of a new past for America, taking over many ingredients from

[1] Indeed, America quickly adopted the Whig interpretation of history, tracing its own love of liberty to its 'Gothic', its Saxon past. See Samuel Kliger, 'Emerson and the Usable Anglo-Saxon Past', *Journal of the History of Ideas* (1955), xvi 476–93.

[2] David Levin, *History as Romantic Art* (Stanford University Press, 1959), 24. 'The minute and unwearied research, the scrupulous fidelity and impartial justice with which you execute your task, prove to me that you are properly sensible of the high calling of the American press – that rising tribunal before which the whole world is to be summoned, its history to be revised and rewritten, and the judgment of past ages to be cancelled or confirmed.' (Washington Irving to Motley, loc. cit.) Also Richard Hofstadter, *The Progressive Historians* (New York, 1968), 15 ff. The 'Whig' interpretation was, however, well established before the romantic historians. See Kliger, op. cit. 457, for a powerful expression of it in 1799.

its old theological past, but also adding to it fresh dimensions. They kept, of course, the sense of special destiny, but they also made subtle use of America's historical situation. They saw it as a remote, empty land where nature reigned supreme. Free from the age-old corruptions of Europe, America had nurtured a tougher, harsher, nobler, purer breed, less sophisticated but more honest. The struggle with nature had developed a true manliness; its beauties, its solitudes, its uncompromising grandeur, whether of mountain or prairie, had drawn forth, indeed created, a noble breed of virile men.[1] This was, of course, largely a

[1] Of course, white men. America's past was white and it was, of course, like England's or Germany's, a racist past. It could be, and was, used to justify slavery, and when that was abolished, it was used to justify the subjection of the blacks. Indeed, the sense of a special white destiny, implicit in America's history, made it easy for the new states of the Middle West to adopt with confidence a rigorous racist policy towards the blacks. The Brahmins too could patronize the blacks and despise them on the same grounds of manifest, historical destiny – and did. The blacks, like the European proletariat, had no past except for a few myths of protest – a Nat Turner for a Robin Hood. The curious exception to this situation is the growing idealization of a certain type of Indian warrior which we find in Fenimore Cooper, Henry Longfellow and others. For the influence of the white past on racist attitudes, see Winthrop D. Jordan, *White Over Black: American Attitudes to the Negro, 1550–1812* (Chapel Hill, 1968); V. J. Voegeli, *Free but not Equal: The Midwest and the Negro during the Civil War* (Chicago, 1968). It is interesting that the last two years have witnessed a determination amongst the blacks to acquire a past of their own. Like many a white past it has little to do with history. An obvious illustration is the elementary schoolbook, *The Freedom Primer*. The same development occurred in Ghana where the murals were painted to show how Ghana had invented

past manufactured for the North-East and West. Yet it was to serve all America well. Its appeal to the farmers of the Middle West is obvious. Yet its strongest attraction was for the New England Brahmins. It enabled them to despise ideologically business, finance and industry, upon which they kept, in practice, so firm a hand. It strengthened the sense of special virtue in their own class in a flooding sea of immigrants and factory workers whom they loathed.[1]

These romantic historians, so close to Sir Walter Scott and Fenimore Cooper, were sensitive, however, to changes taking place in Europe's attitude to the human past. With the breakdown of the all-embracing and simple Christian past, not one but several new interpretations had gained currency in Europe, of which nationalist history of Manifest Destiny, whether crude or subtle, was but one. Many European intellectuals in the seventeenth and eighteenth centuries were more concerned with the problems of human history and institutions that reach across

---

both the alphabet and the steam-engine. There is no need for laughter and none to sneer; all white pasts have made assumptions equally outrageous and for exactly the same purpose – to create both confidence and a sense of special virtue. Indeed, is it less arrogant to claim the steam-engine and the alphabet than 'freedom' and 'liberty' and 'equality' in a society in which there were slave markets? White history is not notable for its clear-eyed vision of things as they were.

[1] It was, of course, by the late nineteenth century, with the growth of a plutocracy and huge industrial working class, to create also a crisis of conscience, perhaps no better demonstrated than in the life and writings of Mark Twain.

national boundaries or racial division. Knowledge of
the sophisticated culture of China on the one hand,
and of primitive tribes on the other, created problems
which were not soluble by the old Christian chronologies of Orosius or Eusebius, although attempts,
and skilful ones, were made. Increasingly after 1660
the old Christian strait-jacket would not do and began
to tear. But its texture proved to be exceptionally
strong, and the Christian past of literal Biblical interpretation lasted, in a social sense – that is amongst tens
of thousands of ordinary men and women – for
many further generations, even though intellectuals
of every kind – scientists, philosophers, sociologists,
legal scholars and historians – tore it into shreds.
Between the late Renaissance and the end of the
seventeenth century, these attacks were strengthened
by developments both in humanistic studies and by
the development of science. A sense of wonder of the
pagan, pre-Christian past dominated the arts and the
sciences; at the same time a seed of hope was bred.
Bodin, Bacon and others argued that man could do
more than recover the intellectual triumphs of
Greece and Rome, and could surpass them, and that
indeed, with printing, the compass and the gun, had
begun to do so.[1] By 1700 this belief had been demonstrated convincingly by the outstanding advances
both in science, technology and the accumulation of
knowledge. And not only demonstrated, but also

[1] J. B. Bury, *The Idea of Progress* (Dover ed., 1955), 37–63.

largely accepted – not everywhere, it is true, but to a degree which would have been impossible in so short a time at any other period of the world's history – thanks to printing, a technological triumph whose impact is constantly underestimated, one might say unrecognized, by the historians of ideas of this period. It was these revolutions – in science, in technology, in geography – which gave the thoughtful Western man a new perception of his past, and, indeed, of the past of mankind, but particularly his own. The past acquired multiplicity, both in time and place. Yet it should be remembered that all scholars were being nurtured in the Christian past, with its intense sense of narrative, its concept of spiritual conflict between good and evil, and with the conviction that good would ultimately triumph because that was God's purpose for the world. It proved easy to secularize these concepts of progress in general non-Christian terms by the idea that, embedded in man's nature, was a capacity for progress. Evil was ignorance; good, reason. As surely as God would triumph over the Devil, so, as surely, would reason triumph over ignorance. By thinking rationally about the world around him he could improve himself and his institutions. However, no scholar believed this to be a simple uninterrupted process. Man was also a concoction of fear, of habit, of superstition; often stupid, often greedy and self-centred; often more concerned with things immediate than with things future. Human nature remained therefore the centre of a struggle. The past, the whole past, pagan, Chinese or Christian, pointed to the growth of rationality, no matter how many setbacks humanity might have encountered. The *philosophes* when they regarded the past were not blind optimists. They were well aware of evil and greed and the plight of men. But they were as convinced as Christians, and perhaps because they all had begun as Christians, that there was a higher destiny for man which his past demonstrated, not only materially, but also morally and socially.[1] Hence the idea of progress pervaded the intellectual world in which the American Romantic historians learned their profession. And as no one believed progress to be linear, historians could choose its torch-bearers, Greeks, Romans, Dutch, Spanish Conquistadors, Protestants and, of course, finally Americans, and so combine a nation's manifest destiny with the fate of mankind.

The concept of progress, very widely accepted by 1800, was to provide a useful tool for ordering the evidence of the new past, vast in time, that geology and archaeology unearthed between 1750 and 1850. Difficulties with the old Christian chronology, bad enough in the days of Buffon, grew tangled as thickets from that day when a Suffolk gentleman,

[1] See Charles Frankel, *The Faith of Reason* (New York 1948), which is the most penetrating of many studies of the idea of progress in the eighteenth century.

Mr Frere, picked up a hand-axe, humanly fashioned, on his estate at Hoxne in Suffolk. It reposed in a gravel stratum that made Archbishop Ussher's definite date, 4004 B.C., utterly ludicrous for the creation of Adam – a date which, it is true, had long been suspect. But visual proof of its inanity had now appeared and soon abounded. The remote past, archaeological as well as geological, littered Europe in Danish bogs, Swiss lakes and Spanish caves.[1] This past acquired an explosive quality such as it had not possessed since the fourth century A.D., when the ancient pagan past had been first demolished and then partly destroyed. Indeed, this crisis of the past was as dramatic and as intellectually disturbing as the destruction of the classical past in China in the twentieth century. A new synthesis was called for. At this time, too, the theory of progress, adumbrated by the philosophers of the Enlightenment, sophisticated and subtle as it was, suffered both at the hands of events and also from the new ideological climate of Romanticism. It was easy to mock this theory as foolishly optimistic – to point to the experience of mankind, with its rise and fall of empires, and to Europe with its revolutions, wars, tyrannies. Both the evidence of the spade and the experience of Europe seemed to demonstrate man's capacity to regress repeatedly in both the civil and moral sphere.

[1] Glyn E. Daniel, *A Hundred Years of Archaeology* (1950); Charles C. Gillispie, *Genesis and Geology* (Harvard, 1951).

Of course, the concept of progress was not lost; that, like a dye, stained all thought and was itself sustained by the obvious, that is by the incredible technical and material growth of Europe. And for coarse and obvious minds such as Macaulay's, this was almost sufficient proof, and he stuck to the theory of progress in its simple forms and combined it with the Whig theory of history, not untouched with a splash of jingoism. In so doing he provided the bulk of the British nation with a usable past, by which they could ease their consciences in the present and look with optimism towards the future.[1]

For other historians and most philosophers this attitude was both too optimistic and too naïve. For some, Hegel provided a more subtle diet; others seized on the social implications of Darwinism crudely understood. Both Hegel and Darwin strengthened the sense of destiny in a national guise and made the past workable in a time of aggressive and competitive imperialism. And Darwinism also took firm root in America, where the complexities of social life created by industrial growth and rapid urbanization made the simple progress theory of the romantic historians increasingly inadequate, at least in the more sophisticated East.[2] Furthermore, America

[1] J. H. Plumb, 'Thomas Babington Macaulay', in *Men and Places* (1963), 250–66.

[2] Richard Hofstadter, *Social Darwinism in American Thought* (Philadelphia, 1944); J. W. Burrow, *Evolution and Society* (Cambridge, 1966), particularly 113–16.

herself was embarking on an aggressive expansionist policy as akin to imperialism as makes no matter, for which the theories of the moral purity of America's past and destiny, as uttered, at times, by Bancroft, Emerson and others, were scarcely appropriate, if not downright jejune. And yet remote as they might seem from the Christian past, both social Darwinism and Hegelianism retained their fundamental dynamic, their belief in development, in change, in an ultimate destiny. Social Darwinism possessed its great popular appeal because it had the advantage of seeming to be rooted in the discoveries of history, anthropology and natural science. Like Christianity, which could be subtle in the hands of a theologian and crude when used by an armed knight, natural selection in the hands of scientists or politicians varied from an intricate hypothetic system to flat assertions. Darwinism, however, gave a powerful structure to the past, seemingly scientific and not mythical, and made it usable in the totally new contexts of early industrial society. It could be applied not only inside a nation but to the world at large. The future it predicted seemed real enough in a world of competitive imperialism – war, violence, the survival of the fittest, which, of course, rulers and governments interpreted, and still do, mistakenly as the strongest.

Darwinism was not the only large-scale general theory that grew from the ruins of the Christian past. For nationalism was but one aspect of nineteenth-century society. Revolutionary socialism prided itself on its universality, and radicals, too, needed an interpretation of the past which they could use in order to make the future which they were forecasting seem inevitable. This, like Darwinism itself, was not a sudden but a slow growth, reaching back into the last decades of the eighteenth century. In 1847 Marx and Engels sketched the socialist past in the *Communist Manifesto* and elaborated it in scores of polemical works.

As is well-known, much here was fused both from the heritage of the Enlightenment and from current philosophy. Methods were taken from Hegel, ideas from Darwin, who refused the dedication to *Das Kapital*. Nevertheless Marx and Engels contributed some novel ideas. This is no place to analyse either the content or the results of Marx's and Engels's achievement. What it did, however, was fundamental. It secularized completely the Christian past but did not obliterate its framework. History was still a narrative, still a conflict between good and evil, still contained a purpose that led it inevitably to an end. The past was still in the service of the future, and its guide. Constant historical analysis is fundamental to revolutionary Marxism. And also it brought, as it was meant to bring, not only hope but also, as the Christian past had done, capacity for sacrifice, for suffering. Changed, perverted, modified in scores of ways, nevertheless Marxism has influenced all radical thought and helped to give radical movements confidence in the future by its interpretation of the past. Yet it was a past that was being used, and not always history. The dialectic was simple, clear, rigid and uniform; all societies had to pass through the same stages of development, and the history of China had to be forced into the same strait-jacket as the history of Europe. And, as with other usable pasts, its intention was moral: not only to create a better world, which would inevitably be born, but also to fortify and discipline individuals, to make them agents of the past and midwives of the future. This secularized and pseudo-scientific past has been the most powerful of all interpretations of the past in modern times, winning millions of adherents, particularly amongst semi-literate and backward peoples, for, like Christianity before it, it reeks with hope. But in the context of the late twentieth century we can observe its weaknesses. Its immediate prognostications have proved as worthless as the prophecies of early Christians. Constant refinement and adjustment have whittled away not only some of its crudities but also undermined much of its simplicity – at least for intellectuals, if not for the illiterate masses. And whatever may happen in China, this interpretation of the past is unlikely to carry the same force with future generations of Russians as it did. There is one other remarkable resonance between the Christian and the Marxist past which is worth comment. The Christians believed that Time would end, when, all men judged, saved or damned, the past would cease to have meaning. Marxist dialectic itself supposes an ultimate end for the practical use of the past. Sooner or later, the Marxists believe, the class conflict will end, the state will wither away. In such circumstances the past will be useless, dead. The past will only exist so long as it is needed for political strategy and tactics, to analyse and forecast conditions in the struggle towards the classless and stateless society. The death of the past is implicit in Marxist ideology. Of course, I do not mean that Marxists expect men and women to be uninterested in history; that would be absurd. Curiosity is bound to flourish, but that is quite different from a socially active past, the past as a weapon in the battle for the future, the past as a process of destiny.

The past as destiny is nearer to death in the non-Marxist world. Few can accept the crude analysis and forecasts of social Darwinianism or the doctrines of Manifest Destiny. For which, amongst these strange communities of men, is fittest to survive, who would care to speculate? And as for Manifest Destiny, few hawks would soar that high. The crude Christian past in which our great-grandparents dwelt is, if not dead, mortally sick. In Western societies we no longer prophecy the future by brooding over the past; it offers so little guidance. We limit the problem in time and use the computer, and get alternative answers. Possible and probable futures can be drawn with some complexity. And prognosis will improve. Much, of course, is still hidden, but few would expect these dark and dangerous places to be illuminated very much by the experience of the past. This, of course, is particularly true of the technologists and scientists who run our lives. Whether it should be so, we must now investigate.

3
THE ROLE
OF HISTORY

THE great Christian past, with its nineteenth-century variations – for they were no more than variations – on that old majestic theme of man's fall and salvation, has collapsed. Rubble, broken arches, monuments crumbling to dust, roofs open to the sky litter this world of thought and loom forebodingly against the horizon. A strange collection of men walk amidst the debris, some full of lamentation, calling for urgent repairs, for an immediate restoration of the old house of the intellect; others climb on to a prominent broken pillar and in self-confident voices explain it all away; others are blind and stumble over the ruins not knowing what has happened. From none of this does humanity derive much comfort. Can this litter of a dead past be cleared away? Can its subtle distortions, or its complex interrelations with all we think and feel, be eliminated from our intellectual heritage. Is to do so desirable, even if possible? And if possible, can man face the future with hope and with resolution without a sense of the past? And if not, can a new past, truer than the old, be manu-

factured to give him a like confidence? These problems, I venture to suggest, lie at the very heart of our
society. And they are problems which no historian
can ignore. For many centuries now history has
burrowed like a death-watch beetle in this great
fabric of the past, honeycombing the timbers and
making the structure ruinous. Now that it has fallen,
can the historian reconstruct a more viable past for
mankind? Or is that like demanding of a surgeon
that he gives up his skill and turns to the problem of
creating life?

So far I have dealt with the past. I have used the
word 'history' as sparingly as I could, but I would have
been happier not to have used it at all – at least, until
this moment. Although historians spend assiduous
lives in its practice and perhaps write more than they
should about its nature and methods, few in the West
are agreed about its purpose or its validity.[1] In
Communist countries, from Poland to China, the
situation is, of course, simpler, for there history and
and the past are but a two-headed Siamese twin.
History is the exegesis of a dogmatic past. It may
refine but it cannot change. But even this situation in Communist Europe and Asia is more appar-
ent than real, more desired than practised, for

[1] The literature on the nature, let alone the philosophy, of history
is vast, and growing. For a quick glance at some of the more notable
pronouncements over the last hundred years, see *The Varieties of
History*, ed. Fritz Stern (New York, 1956), and Hans Meyerhoff, *The
Philosophy of History in our Time* (New York, 1959).

the historical methods of the West, developed over so many centuries, possess an inherent destructive force for all dogmatic assertion. Furthermore, the remodelling of the old Bolshevik past by Stalin, the de-Stalinization of the past by Krushchev, both requiring the immediate past to be rewritten, have undermined dogma and bred scepticism as well as criticism. Serious cracks have appeared in the ideological furniture into which the historian can burrow. Had the Russians been as isolated as Imperial China, such reconstructions of the past might have been possible and become effective for generations; but Russia cannot detach itself from the West. The dogma of history, as now practised in Russia, is unlikely to remain in its present form for many more decades. Soon Russia and her satellites will be facing the problem of a past corroded by the practice of history.

It would, however, be profitless to enter into a philosophic discussion of the nature of history or of its capacity to establish objective truth. The practising historian is like the practising scientist. Just as the latter has no great interest in or use for the philosophy of science, so the active historian is not much concerned with the philosophy of history. He knows history exists and he has been trained in the methods necessary for its investigation. And he knows, too, that increasingly historical studies have been in conflict with the accepted past.

But so that there can be no mistake, it might be as well to define my own position. The aim of history I believe, is to understand men both as individuals and in their social relationships in time. Social embraces all of man's activities – economic, religious, political, artistic, legal, military, scientific – everything, indeed, that affects the life of mankind. And this, of course, is not a static study but a study of movement and change. It is not only necessary to discover, as accurately as the most sophisticated use of evidence will allow, things as they actually were, but also why they were so, and why they changed; for no human societies, not one, have ever stood still. Although we carry within ourselves and within our societies innumerable relics of the past, we have discarded, outgrown, neglected and lost far more. But we have been moulded by Time, all of us, from the naked Negrito in the Malayan forest to the Nobel prize-winners of the Rockefeller Institute. This is a truism, but how this happened poses a problem of exceptional intellectual complexity. The materials for its solution are the debris of Time itself – the records, the artefacts, the monuments, even the landscapes we live in and the languages we speak – materials that are infinite in their number and combination, yet capable of order and interpretation. The historical methods and techniques for the investigation of this process are comparatively young; most of them, such as archaeology, palaeography, topography, sociology, linguistics, demography and the like, have been used by historians for little more than a hundred years. The purpose of historical investigation is to produce answers, in the form of concepts and generalizations, to the fundamental problems of historical change in the social activities of men. These generalizations about societies will, of course, not be immutable but always tentative. They must, however, be as accurate, as scientific, as detailed research and a profound sense of human reality can make them. The historian's purpose, therefore, is to deepen understanding about men and society, not merely for its own sake, but in the hope that a profounder knowledge, a profounder awareness will help to mould human attitudes and human actions. Knowledge and understanding should not end in negation, but in action.[1]

This view of history, which is essentially that of the greatest historian of modern times – Marc Bloch – would, I think, command a considerable measure of assent from working historians. Bloch combined two qualities. He possessed the power to abstract himself from any preconceived notions about the past and to investigate an historical problem with detachment.

[1] There is a common fallacy amongst historians that the pursuit of objectivity must end in negation, e.g. Professor Robert Lynd: 'History, thus voyaging forth with no pole star except the objective recovery of the past, becomes a vast, wandering enterprise'. Quoted by Howard Zinn, 'History as Private Enterprise', in *The Critical Spirit: Essays in Honor of Herbert Marcuse* (Boston, 1967), ed. Kurt H. Wolff and Barrington Moore, Jr, 174.

And yet, detached as he was, his imagination, his creative invention, his sense of humanity infused all that he did. And although it may seem odd, his historical work gained from his wonderful, omnivorous appetite for life that was secure in the delight he derived from living. He loved life – in himself, in others – and because he did his craft of history had to be active. It could not for Bloch be a mere scholarly and imaginative investigation leading nowhere. It had to lead to positive statements about human life, to the acceptance of principles about social living and, I would stress this strongly, create hope. Very many historians who would embrace Bloch's methods with delight would reject the purpose he required historical studies to contain. Indeed, Bloch here was in a very small minority. For an increasing number of historians of the twentieth century, the critical method and the professional debates to which it has given rise are sufficient in themselves. Let us turn, however to the practice of history itself, and glance at Bloch's own work, particularly his remarkable investigation and reconstruction of the life of medieval Europe; in so doing we turn to an extraordinary phenomenon. No other society, no other civilization, has ever given rise to investigations such as these. By the early twentieth century Western civilization had developed a completely new form of history, and Bloch well knew that the science that he practised was very young:

For history is not only a science in movement. Like all those which have the human spirit for their object, this newcomer in the field of rational knowledge is also a science in its infancy. Or to explain more fully, having grown old in embryo as mere narrative, for long encumbered with legend, and for still longer preoccupied with only the most obvious events, it is still very young as a rational attempt at analysis.[1]

Professional history of the twentieth century is as remote from the history produced by our ancestors as modern physics is from Archimedes. Also, as with science, so with history in another aspect. There are more historians alive and practising in the world today than ever before; indeed, there are almost certainly more historians now than the total of all who have ever lived. Hence as a social force their potentiality must be very great, especially so as the vast majority are involved directly in the education of the young. Hence we are presented with a paradox – a past that is in ruins and a proliferating world of historical studies. These are not separate phenomena; they are thoroughly entangled with each other.

To understand the present position, to comprehend the intellectual strength of history and its social weakness, one must turn to the history of history itself, and grapple with the complex problem of why Western European society and its American counterpart began

[1] Marc Bloch, *The Historian's Craft*, trans. Peter Putnam (Manchester, 1954), 13.

to be so concerned to discover historical truth, no matter where the results might lead. Why did history become a pursuit in itself? Even in those years in embryo, to use Bloch's phrase, history was struggling not only towards accuracy, but to analysis, to the description of growth and, in an elementary sense, to the reconstruction of past societies in their own terms.

The contrast between the role of history in China and in the West is illuminating. China, as dynasty followed dynasty, acquired a large historical archive, as diverse and as mountainous as the historical material of Western Europe, and stretching over a longer period of time. Yet Chinese methods of using this material and generalizing about it did not fundamentally change from dynasty to dynasty, and Chinese scholars were using historical materials for the same pragmatic purposes in the early twentieth century as in the T'ang or Han dynasties. Within the tenets of their traditional generalizations they could be subtle and on occasion glimpse the problem of the growth of institutions outside the dynastic context, but Chinese history never developed the process of self-criticism and discovery, the relentless testing of generalization, the purposeful search for documentation to prove hypotheses which marks Western history. In consequence, when traditional Chinese historiography began to collapse in the late nineteenth century, the result was chaos and confusion. Chinese historians, aided and abetted by Western students of their country, snatched at Western generalizations, particularly Marxist ones, and applied them to Chinese data. But this was rather as if the detailed concepts of advanced chemistry were used on a large quantity of freshly discovered biological facts. The generalizations of Western history were the refined end-product of years of patient argument in which generalization and fresh facts had created an ever more sophisticated dialogue. To apply these in any meaningful way to China on the data available was well-nigh impracticable. Once the traditional generalizations were removed, Chinese history collapsed into fragments. The narrative of dynasties remained, of course, but explanation vanished. They possessed neither a usable past nor a core of historical analysis and explanation.[1]

[1] See the most important and suggestive article by Arthur F. Wright, 'On the Uses of Generalization in the Study of Chinese History', in *Generalization in the Writing of History* (Chicago, 1963), ed. Louis Gottschalk, 36–58; also J. Gray, 'Historical Writing in Twentieth Century China: Notes on its Background and Development', in *Historical Writing on the Peoples of Asia: Historians of China and Japan*, ed. W G. Beasley and E. G. Pulleyblank (Oxford, 1961), 186–212. This volume also contains a fascinating essay (pp. 135–66), 'Chinese Historical Criticism: Liu Chih-chi and Ssu-ma Kuang', by E. G. Pulleyblank, which demonstrates the great sophistication of Chinese historiography within its own rigid framework of generalization. Of course, the generalization was no more and no less rigid than that of the Christian West, and the arrangement of sources and the detail contained in them was infinitely greater. But I would maintain that the Chinese were concerned solely with creating an educative past – subtle, complex, highly detailed, accurate in commission, but not history.

Why did history develop in Europe, whereas in China it never extracted itself from the iron grip of the past in the service of the present? The usual answer is to stress the isolation and self-sufficiency of China.[1] But the problem goes deeper than this. China was not without interest in or contact with other civilizations, particularly Japan, Vietnam, Cambodia, Indonesia and India, whose beliefs and social structure differed from her own. And Chinese sages, confident and arrogant as they were about Chinese culture, were not devoid of curiosity.[2] *What closed their minds to the historical problem was its absence.* For the Chinese scholar the past stretched out from his own time like the sea – ruffled here and there by storm and tempest, but limitless. There was no dramatic collapse of a civilization which had lasted for centuries; there was no great revolution in belief that had half obliterated the culture of former times. The area of necessary explanation confronting a Chinese and Western historian was quite different.[3] The European intellectual, even in the fourth and fifth centuries of our era,

[1] Wright, loc. cit. 39.

[2] See two brilliant books by Edward H. Schafer, *The Golden Peaches of Samarkand* (University of California Press, 1963), and *The Vermilion Bird: A Study of T'ang Images of the South* (University of California Press, 1967), which discuss the interest of the Chinese of the T'ang dynasty in Central Asia and the tropical South and the exotics which they produced.

[3] No Chinese historian suffered even the surprise of Herodotus at Thebes when, confronted by three hundred generations of high priests, he was made to realize the youthfulness of Greek society.

had two pasts to contend with. By the time of the Enlightenment he had three. Always in subterranean contact, or overt conflict, there were two others, deeply involved in his own, yet different in interpretation and different, too, in usage of materials – the past of the Jews and the past of Islam. Hence the European's past never possessed the coherence or the unity, the all-embracing certainty of the Chinese. And here lies the key to why Europe could, indeed was bound to, develop critical history. There was in Europe's past no unity; the pagan past could not be obliterated, and the catastrophe of Rome's decline fascinated the curious and created an intellectual problem that insisted, generation after generation, on explanation.

Now problems of conflicting pasts do not necessarily lead to historical methods as we know them, but they do present quite formidable problems which require explanation. The huge output of quasi-historical theology and Church history both in the fourth and sixteenth centuries is an indication of the need to explain the revolution in attitude to the past which took place at these times. And both these critical periods of European ideology deeply influenced the growth of historiography; or, at least, embryos were implanted in the womb of the past which could develop into true history.

The changeover from the pagan to Christian ideology was particularly seminal. The delay of the

Second Coming, the development of an organized, hierarchical Church, the growth of the concept of heresy, and the final marriage between Church and State created a need, in the fourth century, to explain the past in a way which differed profoundly from that employed by pagan historians. The hand of God in the Christian's destiny had to be traced to remote times, back indeed to the Creation; the power of the Church, the supremacy of bishops (and later the authority of the Pope) required proof, historical and documentary proof. Again, the definition of heresy relied on decisions of historical synods and councils; the relations between Church and State, which ranged widely over property and privileges, again needed the authenticity of document. And the result had to be so much more exclusive than pagan history. Christianity was exclusive, yet all-embracing, so the past required explanation or rejection; it could not be simply neglected. And it was this necessity which, as Momigliano has shown us, created a new form – ecclesiastical history – whose first great practitioner was Eusebius. The features of ecclesiastical history which are important in the present context are its documentation and its controversial nature. One did not merely record the annals of the past, or use the past as an illustration of ethics or philosophy; one needed, also, to prove its validity by argument. In the new Christian past, enshrined in ecclesiastical history, which came to dominate European ideology for the next thousand years, there were two vital aspects for the further development of history as we know it; one was the belief in documentary proof, the other was the sense that there was another interpretation, the pagan one, that had to be refuted.[1] Two pasts existed in conflict no matter how victorious the Christian past was with the majority of men.

[1] 'Perhaps we have all underestimated the impact of ecclesiastical history on the development of historical method. A new chapter of historiography begins with Eusebius, not only because he invented ecclesiastical history, but because he wrote it with a documentation which is utterly different from that of the pagan historians': A. Momigliano, 'Pagan and Christian Historiography in the Fourth Century A.D.', in *The Conflict between Paganism and Christianity in the Fourth Century*, ed. A. Momigliano (Oxford, 1963), 92. The whole essay is profoundly important and I am deeply indebted to it. Professor Momigliano stresses the rejection by Christian historians of the pagan past. He points out that the Christians of the fourth century made no serious attempt to provide a Christian version of Livy or Thucydides. 'A reinterpretation of ordinary, military, political or diplomatic history in Christian terms was neither achieved nor even attempted': ibid. 88. And, of course, the whole Pantheon of pagan heroes was rejected. Biography ceased and was replaced by hagiography. No such total rejection of a sophisticated ideology of the past is comparable to this until modern times. The Islamic revolution in Arabia certainly had a profound influence on the Arabs' view of their past, but there was far more continuity. See Julian Obermann, 'Early Islam', in Robert C. Dentan, *The Idea of History in the Ancient Near East* (New Haven, 1955); also Franz Rosenthal, 'The Influence of the Biblical Tradition on Muslim Historiography', in Bernard Lewis and P. M. Holt, *Historians of the Middle East* (Oxford, 1962). And, in any case, the pre-Muslim past of the Arabs was very unsophisticated. Elaborate and coherent pasts which become the prerogative of a band of trained professional scholars can only be found in complex and highly sophisticated societies. For the philosophical naïveté of the historian of medieval India, see P. Hardy, *Historians of Medieval India*

Even in the Dark Ages, the past of Rome and
Greece beckoned. Its salvation lay partly in the preservation and extension of Latin as the language of
belief, administration and culture, and partly in the
sense of loss created by the visible monuments of
former greatness, above all in Rome, but also
throughout Italy, Greece, southern France and parts
of Spain. This old past might be pagan, but it was
undoubtedly impressive. And although the monuments crumbled and decayed, suffering the slow
obliteration of Time, the literature remained, copied
by monks and preserved in monastic libraries, and,
when copied, often revered for its own intrinsic
worth.[1] The old past was never entirely lost; it
survived in sufficient depth to make recovery both
possible and likely. In the darkest times it retained
amongst scholars and writers a tenuous life, even in

(1960), 18–19, 125–31. The same is true of Indonesian history, which
is largely a complex of myths in which some historical facts are
buried. This was quite adequate for the primitive and courtly societies of Indonesia until the present time when the need for a unifying,
socially usable past became keenly felt. See C. C. Berg, 'The Javanese
Picture of the Past', in *An Introduction to Indonesian Historiography*,
ed. Soedjatmoko, Mohammad Ali, G. J. Resink and G. McT. Kahin
(Ithaca, 1965), 87–117. Soedjatmoko's essay on 'The Indonesian
Historian and his Time' is a fascinating discussion of the problems
facing a Western-trained historian confronted by a society with a
very primitive sense of the past. However, no society, primitive or
advanced, has suffered such ideological fractures as Europe.

[1] See R. R. Bolgar, *The Classical Heritage and its Beneficiaries* (Cambridge, 1954), for a brilliant discussion of what the Middle Ages made
of their classical inheritance.

its most secular aspects. It always promoted curiosity and respect, and time and time again enriched philosophy, science, mathematics and geography. Nevertheless, it posed a question – the vast and daunting problem of why this splendid, sophisticated, cultured world had vanished. God's will was one easy and, perhaps, satisfactory answer for the majority of monkish scholars. The more elaborate explanations of St Augustine satisfied the sophisticated, but with the growth of a more secular culture from 1200 onwards, the question could not be so easily answered. Two great periods, two great epochs, began to loom large as cultivated and scholarly men looked back at their past; and with gathering momentum men began to regard the time which stretched between themselves and the ancients as a time of darkness, of barbarism, of obscurity,[1] a process which was not stopped by the Reformation but intensified by it, for the religion itself acquired two pasts – the pure past of the primitive Church and the corrupt past of Rome. Of course, this duality of the past did not immediately lead to the historical method as we know it, but it did posit problems of great com-

[1] Joseph Anthony Mazzeo, *Renaissance and Revolution: The Remaking of European Thought* (New York, 1965), 61: 'Petrarch and his humanist successors . . . were, in fact, able to view the classical past in an historical perspective, as something distant, yet accessible, different, yet intelligible and eminently usable. As the natural landscape that the Renaissance artist painted existed in a mathematically intelligible space, so the ancient world existed for the humanists in a well-defined structured historical space.'

plexity to any historian. At first, the great historians of the Renaissance – Machiavelli and Guicciardini – wished to emulate the ancients, particularly Livy: to divorce history of their own time from the providential and the miraculous and to discover the truths of humanity in the actions of men.[1] Their purpose was basically moral and educative. Also they were primarily concerned with contemporary or near-contemporary history. Good as they were, they were in intention nearer to Thucydides than to ourselves. And yet there was a powerful difference. From the time of Eusebius, records, the written evidence, had acquired immense prestige as validitators of the truth, and the critical use of records for the writing of history had made considerable progress. True, the canons of criticism were often primitive by our standards, but not always. Guicciardini achieved a level of documentation for his *Storia d'Italia* that was almost modern in its range and complexity.[2]

[1] This is, in a sense, only half true of Guicciardini. He describes the portents and miracles – the monstrous births, the sweating images, etc. – which preceded Charles VIII's invasion of Italy, and obviously he believed in God. But within the framework of destiny he attempted a complex and detailed explanation in terms of human character and action. Both Machiavelli and Guicciardini are much closer in attitude to Herodotus, Thucydides, Livy and Tacitus than to their monkish predecessors of the Middle Ages, but some credulity, at least with Guicciardini, lingers powerfully on.

[2] Herbert Butterfield, *The Statecraft of Machiavelli* (1955); also R. Ridolfi, *The Life of Francesco Guicciardini* (1967), 259: 'In the *Storia d'Italia* Guicciardini used documents with a method more rigorous than any had done before him and few did after.'

The concept of a dual past therefore, was clarified and greatly strengthened in the fifteenth century. For the first time there was a sense of anachronism, which can be discerned in painting and illumination as well as in literature. Livy is no longer illustrated by Romans in medieval costume, and Masaccio's apostles wear the toga; Alberti does not use Gothic ornament to decorate his classical villas; Donatello and Brunelleschi deliberately searched in the ruins of Rome for pure forms of the antique.[1] The same desire for purity, to re-achieve the ancient world without the accretions of time, was at work even more strongly in the fields of scholarship. Both philologists and lawyers realized that language and law had changed vastly since the days of Cicero or Justinian. The knowledge that words meant different things at different epochs, that law derived from an historical context, obviously enriched the sense of time in scholars who practised these disciplines. The divergences which they discovered created an acute sense of the duality of the past. This led to absurdities, to the silliness of those Ciceronians who refused to use

[1] On the other hand there is a deliberate Gothicism in Uccello's work. For this see Erwin Panofsky, *Renaissance and Renascences in Western Art* (Stockholm, 1960) and *Studies in the History of Iconography: Humanistic Themes in the Art of the Renaissance* (New York, 1939). Of course, there were bound to be many anachronistic features of religious art, when ignorance of the actual world of the ancients was so widespread. What is interesting is that the attempt was made, which implies the consciousness of a different past. See also J. H. Plumb, *The Renaissance* (1961), 95–96.

any Latin word not to be found in Cicero's works, but even foolishness can propagate seminal ideas. More important and more far-reaching in the effect on the development of history was the furious battle between those lawyers who followed the *mos italicus* and the innovators who preferred the *mos gallicus.* This approach – to attempt to see classical language and law as they were – before time had done its work, was in a most profound sense the beginning of historical criticism. The attempt to discover or verify universal truths, through historical knowledge, was almost as old as man, but the development of historical criticism – to see things as they were in their own time – we owe to the late Middle Ages and the Renaissance. It quickly proved, as it was to remain, dangerous and subversive. A method which could be applied to law and language could be used to test theology or to enquire into the institutions of the Church. After all, Lorenzo Valla was an exceptionally fine lawyer, and one who had attacked the traditional views of Bartolus of Sassoferrato at Pavia with such ferocity that he had been forced to quit the university.[1] Lawyers were amongst the intellectual leadership in criticism of the Church for a generation or so before Luther nailed his theses to Wittenberg's church door, and a vast amount of Protestant propaganda was based on historical criticism of the Church of Rome's

[1] See Myron P. Gilmore, *Humanists and Jurists: Six Studies in the Renaissance* (Cambridge, Mass., 1963), 31–32.

historical claims. Moreover, in a desire to revive the essence of the primitive Church, the same intellectual process is at work that agitated the lawyers of the *mos gallicus* or the Ciceronians. We can discover in grammar, in law, in theology a swelling tide of critical erudition that possessed, as its mainspring, this sense of a duality of the past. And, indeed, there was a further dimension which gradually began to assert itself in men's consciousness of themselves in Time. The ancient world was the world of greatness which they wished to recover. As their disdain for the immediate past deepened, and the sense of their own achievement strengthened, so they began to feel that they belonged to a new age; the great discoveries of America and the East, the revolution in religion, the development in technology, led a few if not many scholars and philosophers to a tentative confidence that they might surpass all that had gone before, that recovery of the past would lead to advance in the future. They felt that this might be best achieved by applying the critical spirit to Nature to see things as they truly were.[1]

This is no place to discuss the deepening preoccupation with scientific enquiry which stimulated so many European scholars of the sixteenth and seventeenth centuries, but it became a factor in the intellectual climate

[1] J. B. Bury, *The Idea of Progress* (Dover ed., 1955), 39-41. Also Geoffroy Atkinson, *Les Nouveaux Horizons de la Renaissance Française* (Paris, 1935), for the effect of geographical knowledge.

of the age and strengthened the new attitude to the past
that was rapidly developing; indeed, these centuries
witnessed an historical revolution in every way as profound as the scientific or the geographical ones. All
were linked. The origin of this revolution in historical
studies can be found in the spirit of historical criticism
in law and philology in the fifteenth century. It was
given great impetus by the invention of printing and
the growth of the study of antiquities. For some time
the number of scholars involved in critical studies
remained very small; tiny bands worked in the universities of Padua or Pavia, or lone scholars, such as
Alciato, who took the message to the universities of
France.[1] As the decades passed, the material for
criticism grew vast – ancient classics, chronologies,
editions of all the Fathers of the Church were published in a never-ending stream. Knowledge was
disseminated and scrutinized; private libraries, far
larger than any the largest monasteries had known,
became by the end of the sixteenth century common-
place. Gentlemen whose ancestors possessed one or
two illustrated books of devotion now owned hundreds of volumes ranging over history, philosophy,
literature, rhetoric, grammar – above all well-edited
editions of the classics, usually Latin, in which Cicero
and Plutarch figured most prominently. This, of
course, was a haphazard process; often scholarship
and the cult of antiquities was a pastime for gentle-

[1] See Gilmore, op. cit. 30–33, 61–86.

manly dilettantes. There was no concerted drive for historical studies in the universities, but preoccupation with the ancient past – its arts, its literature, its coins and artefacts – spread far and wide over Europe in the sixteenth century. This secularization of historical studies is very important. The Church had dominated history throughout the Middle Ages and had been responsible for its interpretation. After 1400, history could be the pursuit of anyone with time and inclination. And here is a notable contrast with developments in the East. China, very much earlier, had developed bureaucratic control of historical materials and interpretation. The new universities of Europe never attempted to bureaucratize history; hence historical criticism had a far freer soil in which to develop, with the result that concentration quickly arose on difficult questions of scholarly interpretation, not only on the validity of chronologies but also on the relation of customs described in the Old Testament with pagan rites and sacrifices A whole world of critical erudition began to develop. Sometimes it settled erratically on curious problems. In the seventeenth century a furious and learned debate broke out concerning the longevity of the patriarchs, where the new scientific attitude seemed to be at sharp variance with holy record.[1] Graver problems were caused by the Flood. As men read more and knew more, the historical

[1] N. Egerton, 'The Longevity of the Patriarchs', *Journal of the History of Ideas* (1966), xxvii 575–84.

improbabilities of a Judaeo-Christian past became more difficult to maintain. Nevertheless historical criticism was more like a woodworm working in the heart of a beam – always active, but rarely seen on the surface. Now and again it punctured a hole, but the vast complex edifice of the Christian past remained intact for the large majority of literate and illiterate Europeans. The scholars themselves had no thought of destroying it; the idea would have filled them with pious horror. They wished to accumulate knowledge, to render it accurate and, some of them, to solve the conundrums their accuracy produced.

Yet the fascination of antiquity, particularly its visible relics, grew steadily; inscriptions, coins, medals were all collected with fervour, catalogued and printed. From the fifteenth century onwards interest in antiquities became one of the dominant themes of scholarship and led to the acquisition by European scholars of a large amount of new historical material. Scholarship became, like European society itself, deeply acquisitive, but acquisition led to knowledge and method, and the same antique spirit found rich pastures not only in the classical world but also in the Middle Ages and in local and national history. In many ways, seventeenth-century scholarship was dominated by the antiquarians whom the philosophers of the Enlightenment dismissed as *les érudits*.[1]

[1] A. Momigliano, 'Ancient History and the Antiquarian', in *Studies in Historiography* (1966), 1–39, for a brilliant summary of the

Both historians and antiquarians increased con-
siderably in number during these centuries. And many
of them preferred to work in a limited and exact field
of scholarship, with the result that available sources
in good texts multiplied. Here the work of the
Maurists and Bollandists, who set about clarifying the
great records of the Church and of Catholic Christianity, was outstanding in range and method.[1] The
spirit of scholarship permeated secular as well as
clerical society. In England it is the age of Parker,
Cotton, Bodley, Dugdale, Wanley, who preserved
so much of the English past and provided some of the
first serious historical criticism in our language.[2]

In the pursuit of erudition, new historical techniques were established – epigraphy, palaeography,
diplomatics and numismatics – as well as edited texts,
dictionaries, catalogues, improved chronologies and
encyclopedias, without which the practice of history
as we know it could never have developed. Yet this

---

growth of antiquarianism after the Renaissance and its effect on the
development of the techniques of historical scholarship.

[1] For the Maurists and Bollandists, see M. D. Knowles, *Trans.
Royal Hist. Soc.*, 5th ser., viii (1958), 147–66, and ibid. ix (1959),
169–92.

[2] David C. Douglas, *English Scholars* (1939); *English Historical
Scholarship in the Sixteenth and Seventeenth Centuries*, ed. Levi Fox
(Oxford, 1956); T. D. Kendrick, *British Antiquity* (1950), and F. Smith
Fussner, *The Historical Revolution* (1962); J. G. A. Pocock's fund-
amentally important *The Ancient Constitution and the Feudal Law*
(Cambridge, 1957).

vast extension of historical literature and of historical knowledge did not lead, initially, to the type of historical understanding which we attempt. Its intention was largely to purify and establish the 'how' of history, not the 'why'. The great works of Mabillon illustrate this point. Here was a scholar of powerful intellect and acute sense of criticism, who established fundamental rules in his *De Re Diplomatica* for sifting the true from the spurious in medieval charters. His editions of the works of St Bernard were not surpassed for centuries. And yet he never asked himself a question of fundamental historical analysis – why medieval society needed, let alone believed, the grotesque legends of its saints or why saints were so plentiful or so necessary. Neither did the Bollandists working steadily through their calendar of saints. They tried to establish the most authentic life of a saint, to refine from the legend the accretions of time. But the whole process of historical change, of why legend? why forgery? why saints? was inconceivable to them. They were not concerned to rewrite history nor to reinterpret the past; they wished to purify and authenticate and make available what existed. Nevertheless they are the fathers of modern historical scholarship as we know it. They proved the value of two things: accumulation of material and critical method.

And they improved, not directly but indirectly, the level of historical discourse. King Lud, the fables of Gildas about the origins of the British people, began to fade from the ordinary historical narrative; similarly, in France kings were no longer descended from the heroes of the Trojan war. Narrative, inexact still by our standards, improved immeasurably. The writing of history itself recovered its critical standards – indeed improved on them. Sarpi was a far greater historian than Livy. And yet, good as the historical scholarship was, and as good as the writing became, history and the past still lived in a curious schizophrenic relationship. Even a scholar as profound as Vico was still locked in historically antique concepts, such as his three ages, which has stronger links with Hesiod than with the historical scholarship of his day. It was not really until the second half of the eighteenth century that historians, notably Gibbon, began to attack the traditional interpretation of the past at its foundations.

Gibbon was not only the heir of the antiquaries and of the great fathers of classical scholarship to whose works he had been constantly drawn since a boy, but also of *les philosophes*, particularly of Bayle, whom he venerated, and of Montesquieu and Voltaire. Their attitude to the past was novel. Bayle and Voltaire, at least, took a sceptical, often malicious, view of the Christian past and all of its works. Voltaire jeered frequently enough at the mole-like activities of *les érudits* and mocked their beliefs. Nevertheless the philosophers were deeply concerned to understand the past in all of its variety and seeming contradiction, searching for laws which would be both rational and convincing. Their interest in historical evidence was largely superficial; it was needed, of course, to underpin an argument or to illustrate a theme, but was not in itself a necessary pursuit in the search for historical truth. Nevertheless their role in the development of historical studies was profound and, for Western society, deeply original. They were attempting to reconstruct the past in non-Christian terms and they were trying, for the first time, to explain the destiny of man by his own nature.[1] At the same time, their purpose was educative, but in the broad, not the precise, sense. The main aim was the understanding, not a mere realizing, of man and his past. Gibbon combined within himself both attitudes. He valued knowledge for its own sake, yet he was aware that erudition could not be an end in itself. History needed to be philosophic and purposeful. But the history of what?

Gibbon's indecision, recorded in his *Journal*, about the subject of his life's work is fascinating and illustrates the basic theme of this chapter to perfection. He considered for some time a variety of subjects, from a life of Sir Walter Raleigh, a history of the Third Crusade to the foundation of the Swiss

[1] See P. Gay's most illuminating work, *The Enlightenment: The Rise of Modern Paganism* (New York, 1966).

Republic. They stirred his imagination, but wisely he dropped them. Raleigh was too parochial, the Swiss demanded a knowledge of German language and literature that he was not prepared to undertake.[1] But all these excuses were rationalizations. They posed great historical problems – the Swiss a major one – as did the history of the Medicis with its conflict of cultures, which he considered for a while. He was, however, drawn inevitably to the great problem of European history and the duality of its past. Indeed, his life had largely been a preparation for this work, long before he made his famous journey to Rome. Yet it was in Rome that Gibbon found the image that is a key not only to his own work, but also to the development of historical studies in Europe. He writes in his *Autobiography*:

> It was at Rome, on the 15th of October, 1764, as I sat musing amidst the ruins of the Capitol, while the bare-footed friars were singing vespers in the Temple of Jupiter, that the idea of writing the decline and fall of the city first started to my mind.[2]

[1] Gibbon remained attached to this idea and wrote an introductory piece about Switzerland. His preoccupation is not surprising, for the success of Switzerland in achieving and maintaining its independence presents a curiously difficult problem of historical understanding. Everything that makes for social and political stability would seem to be absent – geography, language, economic integration, religion, or even a common social structure. Yet Switzerland survived, prospered, avoided revolution. Why? The problem still awaits its historian. Gibbon had an unerring instinct for major problems, but luckily chose the largest.

[2] Edward Gibbon, *Autobiography* (Oxford, 1907), 169.

Here, in succinct symbolism – the bare-footed friars, the Temple of Jupiter – Gibbon placed in juxtaposition the two great cultures that Western Europe had experienced, the question that had haunted scholars of two centuries or more, the condition which had produced the inner dynamic of so many historical studies of which Gibbon was the heir. He never forgot his debt to the scholars, to the masters of historical criticism and method who made his work possible. What Gibbon did, however, was to absorb their work and make it a part of historical literature for all time. After Gibbon, history was fully fledged. The success of his book brought, as did the works of other historians of the Enlightenment, a new depth to the understanding of European history amongst the educated élite. As with Voltaire or Hume, Gibbon interpreted history in purely human terms. Of course, he made moral judgments and he stressed the effects of chance. But his moral judgments were those of men, not God, and his chance was purely human, not a great external force, not *Fortuna* playing grimly with the lives of men. History had to be understood in human terms, be motivated by human forces; follies and iniquities abounded, but they were neither the result of ignoring the gods nor of original sin. Gibbon raised the writing of history to a new level. He was aware, more acutely than any of his predecessors, both of its possibilities and its limitations. He sought a detached and truthful past, free from

preconception or the idea of inherent purpose. Yet
his detachment was infused with a warm and
generous attitude to mankind in spite of its immeasur-
able follies and iniquities. Gibbon frequently spoke of
the candour of history, because it could display, not
truths about the universe, or immutable laws of
social development, but merely the truth of ourselves
as living human beings.[1] History contained causes
and events, not laws or systems. And yet Gibbon did
not believe he was writing merely to entertain.
History possessed a purpose and this was to deepen
experience, to make men wiser about themselves and,
also, about the social processes in which they were
necessarily involved. After all, he wanted to explain
the greatest cataclysm of European history.

But Gibbon stood in lonely detachment; most of
the philosophic historians of the Enlightenment
wished to wring more than he did from their study of
history, to find immutable laws of historical change
and development. They discovered their overall
design in Progress, about which they grew both
rhapsodic and optimistic. Gibbon shared little of their
enthusiasm. He did, however, give a highly qualified
assent to their general proposition that the condition
of mankind had improved. To this we will return
later.

Gibbon had demonstrated that historians could

[1] Per Fuglum, *Edmund Gibbon: His View of Life and Conception of
History* (Oslo, 1953), 41.

rewrite the history of antiquity with a wealth of detail and knowledge that surpassed classical historians. Herodotus, Thucydides, Livy, Tacitus and the rest were no longer the occupants of Olympian heights, unattainable by moderns. And scholars turned to the history of Greece and Rome with a new vigour. But the historical ferment went deeper. Through the discoveries of archaeology, Time itself was given a vast extension towards the close of the eighteenth century. The decipherment of the Rosetta Stone, the quickening pace of discovery in Assyria and Babylonia, the deepening knowledge of India and China brought a new sense of the diversity of man's past and enlarged the problems of history. Nor did erudition wane, indeed it waxed. New archives, particularly medieval archives, became available in the early nineteenth century. The spread of Maurist and Bollandist methods to the great national sources of history in Germany, in France and in England made history not only a widespread profession but also a highly technical craft.[1] Against this huge deluge of material, historians struggled manfully. Leopold von Ranke still hoped to write a Universal History; indeed, he settled down to write it at the age of eighty-six. He wrote in the 1860s that

In my opinion, we must work in two directions:

[1] See David Knowles, *Great Historical Enterprises* (1963), 65-134; also Herbert Butterfield, *Man on His Past* (Cambridge, 1955), particularly pp. 75-85.

the investigation of the effective factors in historical events and the understanding of their universal relationship . . .

The investigation of a single detail already requires profound and very penetrating study. At the present time, however, we are all agreed that the critical method, objective research, and synthetic construction can and must go together. Historical research will not suffer from its connection with the universal: without this link, research would become enfeebled, and without exact research the conception of the universal would degenerate into a phantasm.[1]

Ranke's intention is still Gibbon's – to combine the most exact erudition with philosophic history.

The professional historian, as the nineteenth century progressed, was forced into narrower and narrower fields of study, and often his studies were still the servants of an overall concept of the past. Indeed, there is no outstanding historian of the nineteenth century who did not accept a large structural interpretation of the destiny of man, and usually of his nation too. The task, however, grew ever more difficult. And the twentieth century brought a change. Time and time again large-scale and small-scale assumptions about the purpose or meaning of history were sharply attacked. Professional historians began increasingly to reduce their generalizations to the professional areas of their interest. Did the Norman

[1] Fritz Stern (ed.), *The Varieties of History*, 62.

Conquest introduce feudalism into England? Was slavery a cause of the American Civil War? Did the *philosophes* help to provoke the French Revolution? Specialization confined itself to professional and not philosophic concepts. As in the seventeenth century, erudition dominated historical studies; the pursuit of scholarship became more important than the interpretation of history. Periodically, the professional historian lifted his head and tried to make up his mind what could or could not be derived from historical study. His answers expressed doubt, uncertainty, perhaps even bewilderment, and many thought it better not to embark on generalizations as perilous and as disputatious as these. After all, the debris of the past, shovelled wholesale into thousands of libraries and national and local record offices, provided material for work for tens of thousands of professional historians who were content to reduce it into some kind of order in fields of ever increasing specialization. Ten years of the history of Seattle or Sienna could provide a lifetime's work and a lifetime's academic career. And, on occasion, rightly so; for such studies in the hands of a professional historian of ability can help to solve technical and scholarly problems of great importance. After all, Bloch's own work was deeply rooted in local history.

Hence, history tended to become in the twentieth century, for the majority of its practitioners, a study for professionals by professionals. The purpose of history was limited; it trained the mind in criticism and in judgment, satisfied curiosity and made the wise wiser. What they would not allow was the old philosophic attitude of the Enlightenment, that history should interpret the destiny of mankind. This attitude of limited objectives and intentions has been common to those historians who have attempted, during the last sixty years, to keep history as a part of general culture, as well as of highly professional scholars who are concerned with the rigours of historical method. And, indeed, even today this is as far as the majority of historical writers and historical scholars would go in giving meaning and purpose to history. The business of the historian is to make sense of the past.[1] That is his primary task, but it is far from simple, for the complexities of historical forces are very intricate and their elucidation never easy. Hence it is natural for the professional historian to limit his field and concentrate his powers. He is likely to achieve greater mastery and deeper understanding, even though his vision in the terms of the history of mankind may be very limited.

---

[1] Richard Pares, *The Historian's Business and Other Essays* (Oxford, 1961), 10: 'The sense [of the past] that historians make is an increasingly complicated sense. It may perhaps be suggested that professional classes always create complications in order to make themselves indispensable. But I think that such an explanation would do the professional historians less than justice. It is a matter of scientific conscience. The historical process is very complicated: it has its laws and its uniformities, but it can only be explained in terms of itself.'

This is, of course, a highly defensible attitude. Limited it may be, but it is sound, sensible and cautious. It has commanded respect over the last two centuries. The professional purpose is to understand, neither more nor less. This attitude can be traced back to the Enlightenment, to Herder who, concerned as he was with moral judgment in history, nevertheless realized that empathy was essential to the historian's task. Empathy, imagination, the attempt to place oneself in an historic situation and into an historic character without pre-judgment, rose in public favour throughout the nineteenth century. Indeed, Marc Bloch in the twentieth called 'understanding' the beacon light of our studies.[1] However, this restricted view still leaves unanswered the deeper question – the understanding of what? A human character, an event in time, the nature of an institution, of the reasons for belief? The progression rises. Dare it lift to the process of history itself? It would seem not. Bloch, unlike Ranke, could not contemplate a universal history. By his day, history itself had rendered this impossible. Or rather, not impossible, but intellectually useless. To the trained historian, erudition by its very bulk had obliterated the possibility of that universal synthesis so much desired by Ranke. The historian's business may be to make sense of the past, but only of his own patch and not the vast panorama that stretches back to the beginning of time.

[1] Bloch, *The Historian's Craft*, 143.

And so we come to the heart of the paradox. History began because scholars perceived a problem which faced no other civilization – the problem of the duality of Europe's past, its conflicting ideologies and of their different interpretations of human destiny. Once historical criticism developed, the Christian explanation of the past could not maintain its supremacy. It slowly collapsed under criticism, but just as slowly and just as surely did the interpretations which replaced it – the concept of progress, the manifest destinies of competitive nationalism, social Darwinism, or dialectical materialism. History, which is so deeply concerned with the past, has, in a sense, helped to destroy it as a social force, as a synthesizing and comprehensive statement of human destiny.

Because of this, most historians in this century have avoided any attempt to explain the history of man. This has been left to the journalists, the prophets or the philosophers, but some of those who have attempted it acquired great popular success. H. G. Wells, Oswald Spengler and Arnold Toynbee, who sought to mould history into a meaningful past, secured millions of readers but the almost universal condemnation of historians. Yet the reception of their books points to the need of ordinary people, as well as to the difficulty of fulfilling it.[1] Although the past manufactured by

[1] Apart from the excellent and stimulating world history of William H. McNeill, *The Rise of the West* (Chicago, 1963), the most successful attempts have been made by archaeologists – Carleton S. Coon and Gordon Childe.

his ancestors will no longer do, it would seem that man in the West still seeks a meaningful past, one which will confer as much significance on his life as the Marxist past does for those who can believe in it. Can historians fulfil this need? And is it their rightful task?

The historian, I believe, has a twofold purpose. He must pursue and test the concepts with which he deals. And because of the amount of material and its complexity, these concepts are likely to be limited in time. Much of his life must be spent, therefore, working with, and writing for, fellow professionals. These, as yet, are very early days for exact, professional history. But this cannot be the historian's sole *raison d'être*. Some would argue that the training which experience, even a short experience, gives in the techniques of historical study is a sufficient argument for its existence. This is the old argument for classical studies in a new guise. It is, of course, true that historical study does exercise memory, capacity for argument and clarity of expression. And it is excellent that it should do so, but there are plenty of academic disciplines which can do this, perhaps better than history.[1] The study of history can, of course, and does extend human experience in a peculiarly vivid way, but so do literary studies, so should sociology or

[1] On the argument for classical studies as a training for the intellect, see M. I. Finley, 'Crisis in the Classics', in *Crisis in the Humanities*, ed. J. H. Plumb (1964), 18-19.

anthropology or the study of politics.[1] Again, this is in no way peculiar to history. The combination of all these virtues would justify a minor academic discipline and fulfil a minor social role in satisfying curiosity and gratifying nostalgia. History as entertainment, whether of the intellectual or of the romantic housewife, would persist. If this, however, were all that a study of history could do, no one would insist that it fulfils a vital and major social role. Yet if the past is allowed to die, or, having died, a new one fails to be conceived, that will be the fate of history. Its place as the interpreter of man's destiny will be taken by the social sciences.

In many ways the historian of today is in the position of the historian of the Enlightenment. He cannot accept the interpretation of the past of his immediate ancestors or even of the mass of society in which he lives. Crude ideological interpretations, Marxist or nationalist, conservative or liberal, religious or agnostic, providential or progressive, cyclical or linear, are a violation of his discipline and an offence to his knowledge. Many historians, therefore, have taken refuge in the meaninglessness of history, in the belief that history can only make a personal or neutral statement; it is a game for professional players

[1] 'Its true value is educational. It can educate the minds of men by causing them to reflect on the past': G. M. Trevelyan, *Clio: A Muse and other Essays* (new impr. 1949), 147. See also G. R. Elton, *The Practice of History* (Sydney, 1967), 48–50.

who make the rules. Others, more conservative, have taken refuge in its providential nature. The Christian myth dies hard. We need again a compulsive sense of the value of man's past, not only for ourselves as historians, but also for the world at large.

The historians of the Enlightenment could discover with delirious joy the antique past that beckoned them in Greece and Rome; the multiplicity of historical worlds that rose above their intellectual horizon – Egypt, Persia, India, China – gave them new stimulus, fresh ideas, and a deep sense of recovery, of escape into a fresher, more viable historical understanding. Alas, such an experience cannot revitalize the historian of this century.[1] There are no new pasts to discover. They are all exposed and all peopled by professional experts, digging in their minute concessions in the hope of finding a new sherd. The very limitations of professional historical study make it difficult for historians to deal with any messages that might be derived from the vista of man's past, even if he believed in them. He does not look for them. He does not wish to lift his eyes from what he can see with clarity to what may be baffling, obscure and misleading. Philosophical history is at a discount, and antiquarianism, transmuted into scholarship, triumphs. After two world wars, after Hitler and Hiroshima, after the brutalities of Stalin and the sad failures in Africa, in India, in Indonesia, historians cannot help

[1] Gay, *The Enlightenment: The Rise of Modern Paganism*, 46–47.

but look at the immediate, as well as the distant, past with foreboding and with pessimism. But blind optimism has rarely been the fault of the perceptive historian; Voltaire and Gibbon, the greatest historians of the Enlightenment, were conscious enough of the follies, the iniquities, the stupidities of mankind. But they were sufficiently detached to qualify their pessimism and to use a balanced judgment. To them the gains made by mankind were obvious and remarkable. They still are. Any historian who is not blindly prejudiced cannot but admit that the ordinary man and woman, unless they should be caught up in a murderous field of war, are capable of securing a richer life than their ancestors. There is more food in the world, more opportunity of advancement, greater areas of liberty in ideas and in living than the world has ever known: art, music, literature can be enjoyed by tens of millions, not tens of thousands. This has been achieved not by clinging to conservative tradition or by relying on instinct or emotion, but by the application of human ingenuity, no matter what the underlying motive might be. The great extension of rationalism has been a cause and a consequence of this development. In field after field, rationalism has proved its worth. It still has vast areas left to conquer in politics and social organization which may prove beyond its capacity, owing to the aggressive instincts built so deeply into man's nature. Nevertheless, the historian must stress the success, as well as point out the failure. Here is a message of the past which is as clear, but far more true, than the message wrung from it by our ancestors. The past can be used to sanctify not authority nor morality but those qualities of the human mind which have raised us from the forest and swamp to the city, to build a qualified confidence in man's capacity to order his life and to stress the virtues of intellect, of rational behaviour. And this past is neither pagan nor Christian, it belongs to no nation and no class, it is universal; it is human in the widest sense of that term. But this past must not be too simple. Just as the Christian past stressed the complexity of the battle between good and evil, so should the historian's past dwell on the difficulties which have faced those who have fought for intellectual and moral enlightenment. Nor need we gloss their motives. The historian's duty is to reveal the complexities of human behaviour and the strangeness of events. The past which mankind needs is no longer a simple one. Experience as well as science has made the majority of literate men aware of the vast complexity of human existence, its subtle interrelations. What, however, is becoming less and less stressed is the nature of the past, not only its successes, but also the shadows it casts across our lives. History, the dimension of Time, is ignored too frequently by sociologists, economists, politicians and philosophers; even theologians wish to escape from its clutches.

Any past serviceable to society, therefore, must be

complex even though its base may be simple. That simple base I have described above. It is to me the one truth of history – that the condition of mankind has improved, materially alas more than morally, but nevertheless both have improved. Progress has come by fits and starts; retrogressions are common. Man's success has derived from his application of reason, whether this has been to technical or to social questions.[1] And it is the duty of the historian to teach this, to proclaim it, to demonstrate it in order to give humanity some confidence in a task that will still be cruel and long – the resolution of the tensions and antipathies that exist within the human species. These are limited objectives. Historians can use history to fulfil many of the social purposes which the old mythical pasts did so well. It can no longer provide sanctions for authority, nor for aristocratic or oligarchical élites, nor for inherent destinies clothed in national guise, but it can still teach wisdom, and it

---

[1] I do not, of course, believe in a simple dichotomy between reason and unreason. Reason can bolster folly, lead to absurdity and employ itself in the most dangerous ways. It is reason, controlled on the one hand by facts, by experiment and by experience, and energized on the other by man's deepest biological instincts to increase and protect his kind, that has led to success. (Nothing would unify mankind with greater alacrity than an attack from outer space.) No historian can consider the triumphs of rationality to have been easily secured, nor free from the admixture of many other motives. On the other hand, man's rationality, his capacity to think about himself and his environment and to communicate his thoughts is obviously his most precious gift, and makes him unique in the animal world.

can teach it in a far deeper sense than was possible when wisdom had to be taught through the example of heroes.

Because of the complexities of its dual past – pagan and Christian – because of the collapse of the Roman Empire, because the Christian past after the Reformation became multiple, because of the impact of great civilizations with a past of their own, because of the discovery in Europe of the huge time-span of man's existence in the world, Western society has been forced not only to study but to accept the fact of social change, of not only the complexity and variety of human existence, but also of its restless social movement in time. As soon as history began to free itself from the past, it was this aspect which drew the best minds to history. It is as true of Gibbon as of Marx, of Michelet as of Bloch. And here lies the greatest contribution that the historian can make. History can teach all who are literate about the nature of social change; even to tell the mere story of social change would be a valuable educational process in itself and help to fulfil a need in present society of which we are all aware. Of course, there will not be agreement; historians will speak with different voices. This no more matters than the lack of unity in wisdom literature did in the past. The importance lies in the nature, the cogency, the presentation of argument. We need to teach people to think historically about social change, to make them alert to the cunning of history which, as Lenin emphasized, always contains a quality of surprise. We must add the depth of time to studies which so singularly lack it. And it should be remembered that history is constantly growing in insight and probing ever deeper into questions which affect our daily lives. The knowledge of the mechanics of historical change is far more profound than it was two generations ago. But much of the professionalism of history remains professional; in spite of the huge output of paperback histories, the results of professional history are not conveyed with the emphasis and cogency that society needs. The historians have, very rightly, been active agents in the destruction of the past to which society has so frequently turned to acquire either confidence or justification or both. This critical, destructive role is still necessary; illusions about the past, even in professional circles, are abundant enough, but the historian, as with other members of society, is being freed from the trammels of the past by the changes in society itself. Paradoxically, what allows the sociologist to ignore the past, enables the historian to see it more clearly. Hence the historian's opportunity is similar, although far from identical, to that of the philosophers of the Enlightenment. They too were slipping off the shackles of the past, destroying its pretensions and its follies, but they also attempted to create out of the debris a more extended, a more rational, a more detached sense of human destiny. And so by his writings, by his thinking, even by his example, the historian today should be similarly engaged.

The old past is dying, its force weakening, and so it should. Indeed, the historian should speed it on its way, for it was compounded of bigotry, of national vanity, of class domination. It was as absurd as that narrow Christian interpretation which Gibbon rightly scorned. May history step into its shoes, help to sustain man's confidence in his destiny, and create for us a new past as true, as exact, as we can make it, that will help us achieve our identity, not as Americans or Russians, Chinese or Britons, black or white, rich or poor, but as men.

INDEX OF NAMES